The short guide to social policy

Second Edition

John Hudson, Stefan Kühner and Stuart Lowe

First edition published in 2008
Second edition published in Great Britain in 2015 by

Policy Press
University of Bristol
1-9 Old Park Hill
Bristol BS2 8BB
UK
+44 (0)117 954 5940
pp-info@bristol.ac.uk
www.policypress.co.uk

North America office:
Policy Press
c/o The University of Chicago Press
1427 East 60th Street
Chicago, IL 60637, USA
t: +1 773 702 7700
f: +1 773-702-9756
sales@press.uchicago.edu
www.press.uchicago.edu

British Library Cataloguing in Publication Data
A catalogue record for this book is available from the British Library.

Library of Congress Cataloging-in-Publication Data
A catalog record for this book has been requested.

ISBN 978 1 44732 568 0 paperback

Cover design by Policy Press.
Front cover image kindly supplied by www.alamy.com
Printed and bound in Great Britain by Hobbs, Southampton
Policy Press uses environmentally responsible print partners.

Contents

List of tables, figures and boxes

Tables

Figures

Boxes

General abbreviations

€	the euro (European currency)
ALMP	active labour market policy
AUS$	Australian dollars (currency of Australia)
DKK	Danish kroner (currency of Denmark)
EU	European Union
EUROSTAT	The statistical office of the European communities
GDP	gross domestic product (a measure of economic output that represents the total size of a nation's economy)
ICVS	International Crime Victims Survey
ILO	International Labour Organisation
IMF	International Monetary Fund
NZ$	New Zealand dollars (currency of New Zealand)
OECD	Organisation for Economic Co-operation and Development
PISA	Programme for International Student Assessment
QUANGO	quasi-autonomous non-governmental organisation
SEK	Swedish krona (currency of Sweden)
TANF	Temporary Assistance for Needy Families
UN	United Nations
UNDP	United Nations Development Programme
UNESCO	United Nations Educational, Scientific and Cultural Organization
UNODC	United Nations Office on Drugs and Crime
UNICEF	United Nations Children's Fund
UNICRI	United Nations Interregional Crime and Justice Research Institute
US$	US dollars (currency of the US)
WHO	World Health Organization

Country abbreviations in charts

Each chapter includes a number of charts comparing social policy across countries. For presentational reasons, we have limited each chart to 20 countries/cases, meaning that the charts do not provide as comprehensive view as would be possible with larger pages, but we have endeavoured to use a wide range of different countries in the charts. We use the standard international three-letter classifications rather than full country names in the charts, again, to save space. A list of the country codes used in the charts is as follows.

ARG	Argentina	IRN	Iran (Islamic Republic of)
AUS	Australia	ISL	Iceland
AUT	Austria	ITA	Italy
BEL	Belgium	JPN	Japan
BRA	Brazil	KOR	Republic of Korea
CAN	Canada	LSO	Lesotho
CHE	Switzerland	MEX	Mexico
CHL	Chile	MWI	Malawi
CHN	China	NLD	Netherlands
CZE	Czech Republic	NOR	Norway
DEU	Germany	NZL	New Zealand
DNK	Denmark	POL	Poland
ESP	Spain	PRT	Portugal
EST	Estonia	RUS	Russian Federation
FIN	Finland	SGP	Singapore
FRA	France	SVK	Slovakia
GBR	United Kingdom of Great Britain and Northern Ireland	SVN	Slovenia

GBR (E&W)	United Kingdom (England and Wales only)	SWE	Sweden
GHA	Ghana	THA	Thailand
GRC	Greece	TUR	Turkey
HUN	Hungary	UK	United Kingdom (GBR in charts)
IDN	Indonesia	US	United States of America (USA in charts)
IND	India	USA	United States of America
IRL	Ireland	ZAF	South Africa

Preface

This textbook arose from the demand of our students at the University of York for a concise, straightforward and clear account of the subject matter of Social Policy and, in particular, the requests of our overseas students who often came to us with questions not only about social policy but also about why so many of their introductory textbooks excluded consideration of any case but the UK.

We were quickly able to show all of our students that Social Policy is an interdisciplinary subject that draws on the knowledge base and concepts of the core social sciences with a focus on the analysis of social problems. After this, the perennial burning question remains: 'What is social policy'? The answer to this is that there are many different definitions and explanations of the subject but when forced by our students to make a decision about where they might best begin, we have increasingly felt that going 'back to basics' offers a good starting point. Our short guide to social policy here focuses on the 'pillars of the welfare state' and echoes the subject in its earliest days of development in the UK, following the setting up of the National Health Service, the state education system, a universal social security system, a massive programme of state housing and a commitment to full employment, all the product of the aftermath of the Second World War, when people expected benefits from the trauma, losses and struggle of war. People were promised a new society and out of the ashes rose the 'welfare state'. While being aware that this apparently simple and even naive solution is itself full of pitfalls and would be unlikely to satisfy many of our colleagues, who might well approach the subject very differently, seen from the perspective of students brand new to the subject, the demand for a short overview of some key building blocks is perfectly understandable.

However, while we take our inspiration from the British case, we have tried to broaden the scope of our reflections here by drawing on examples and evidence from over 60 countries. While our writing still betrays our Western European mindset, we have tried hard to offer a less ethnocentric treatment of the subject matter of Social Policy here, not least because we believe that there is much to be gained from reflecting on how social policies differ across nations. Indeed, we have discovered from our students that, in many ways, the UK 'welfare state' is quite odd and the assumption in much of the literature that the 'Beveridge model of welfare' is a kind of default against which other countries might be judged and compared is mistaken. Looking comparatively helps us to see our own countries more clearly and to recognise that one key dimension of the subject of 'Social Policy' ought to be a comparative analysis.

As an introductory text, this book is mostly descriptive, but it does have an implicit, inner, theoretical structure that is central to its approach: each chapter has a common set of headings and themes and so analyses the core pillars of welfare in a more systematic manner than is often the case in introductions to the subject. While the pillars of welfare are quite different from each other in what they do, we feel that it is still possible to analyse them through a common conceptual lens. Indeed, we believe that theory is key to further understanding, and in the final chapter, the whole tone changes to become much more intentionally conceptual, where Social Policy theory is upfront, acting as a springboard for readers to then move up a gear and broaden their own thinking about this fascinating and immediately urgent subject matter.

All three of us would like to take the opportunity here to thank a number of people who have helped us in assembling the book. The staff at Policy Press have been immensely supportive, as ever, particularly Emily Watt and Victoria Pittman, who provided encouragement to be innovative in taking forward this second edition and ensured that we turned an idea for a new text into reality. Along with Emily and Victoria at Policy Press, Applification played a central role in helping us think through how the book might interact with digital content in this second edition, and, indeed, there would be no accompanying app without their work. Several anonymous referees also gave up valuable time to offer advice about the book, as did our colleagues Kate Brown and Daniel Horsfall at York. Any errors and omissions naturally remain our own. Finally, we would like to offer thanks to the many students, who it has been our great pleasure to teach and who often become our friends, for their support. Even though they may not know it, their encouragement to commit our ideas to paper is the main reason for this text.

John Hudson, Stefan Kühner and Stuart Lowe
York, March 2015

1

introduction

||||||||||||||||||||||||||||||||||||||||||||||||||||||||||||||||||||||||||||||||||||||||||||||||||||||||||||||||||||||||||||||||||||||||||||||||

The ubiquity of social policy

Turn on the TV news, pick up a newspaper, visit a news agency website or scan the blogosphere and you will inevitably hear about social policy issues almost instantly. On 6 March 2015, we sat down to write this introduction and spent an hour or two browsing websites and newspapers from around the world. In so doing, we repeated an exercise conducted for the first edition of this book on 5 October 2007. As then, this was a randomly chosen day, yet the sheer number of social policy-related stories we came across clearly illustrated the fundamental importance of social policy. What is more, the controversies embedded in those stories demonstrated in a very human way the reason why social policy engages people in intense debate so readily, even if they often do not realise that 'social policy' is the subject of so many of their everyday conversations. Such was the number of stories we found that we can only give you a small flavour of them here.

One of the starkest stories we found in October 2007 came from the US, where policy makers were bitterly divided over proposals to increase the number of children covered by health insurance. Just days after 12-year-old Deamonte Driver had died because his family could not afford treatment for a tooth infection, politicians from both main political parties voted to extend coverage to families. President Bush, however, vetoed the reforms on the grounds that they created undue state interference in the healthcare market. By 6 March 2015, some of the major gaps in heathcare coverage had been closed by President Obama's reforms, but the *New York Times* reported that the US Supreme Court were due to begin hearing a case that might see millions of people lose healthcare subsidies. Their own analysis suggested that Obama's Affordable Care Act had reduced the proportion of the US population without health insurance from 18% to 10% but that the Supreme Court case could see this gain rolled back and push the figure to 13%. Healthcare was a matter of debate in many other countries that day too. In the UK, the government was under pressure to review hospital targets after an influential think tank suggested that the government's 'micromanagement' of accident and emergency services had undermined patient care. In Australia, auditors criticised the government for the handing of its multi-billion-dollar contract with drug companies, arguing that planned savings in pharmaceutical spending worth hundreds of millions of dollars had failed to materialise because of administrative deficiencies.

Employment issues featured prominently in the news in many countries. In Turkey, it was reported that newly released figures showed that unemployment in 2014 had reached just under 10% of the workforce, a higher figure than previously estimated and an increase in the rate for 2013. In the Netherlands, it was reported that the economy was continuing to grow, but there was concern that the growth was not likely to reduce unemployment as rapidly as had previously been estimated, the unemployment rate standing at 8.1% and forecast to drop only marginally to 7.9% over the coming year. In the US, meanwhile, there was better news in terms of unemployment: *The Wall Street Journal* reported that the unemployment rate was dropping, but they noted concern over slow wage growth and reported fears that the unemployment rate remained higher than hoped, at some 5.5%.

There were many concerns about social security programmes, such as pensions and unemployment benefits. In Bulgaria, ongoing debate about pension reform was turning into a political crisis as disagreements between different parties forming the government produced political deadlock. In the US, there were reports that that funding for disability programmes was at risk of running out, with major cuts in benefits likely if politicians failed to act quickly. In the UK, the government suggested that child benefits should be limited to only three children as a cost-saving measure; at the same time, it was reported that cuts to social security that had already taken place in the UK had hit single-parent families particularly hard. In Australia, meanwhile, it was reported that the government were under attack from the opposition Labor Party for implementing cost-saving cuts to pensions that were not needed because the schemes were financially sustainable before the cuts were made.

Education was a focal point of debate in many countries. It was reported that the Mexican government's education reform agenda was struggling to meet its goals as the government's confrontational stance towards teachers viewed to be performing inadequately had produced a stand-off that threatened to derail the ambitious schools improvement agenda. Conflicts between government and educators were also an issue in Myanmar as police arrested demonstrators opposed to an education bill that they said placed too much control over universities into the hands of government. In Singapore, meanwhile, a different narrative appeared to be playing out as *The Straits Times* reported that the government had responded to requests for additional funding to support students with complex needs.

Housing pressures were also evident in very many countries. In the *South China Morning Post*, a commentator argued that expanding home ownership would be an ideal way to boost retirement incomes because it would enable people to build up assets that they could use in later life. By contrast, a lead story in the *Sydney Morning Herald* was that the leader of one of the states was promising to 'supercharge' the building of new houses if he was re-elected in order to address growing housing shortages and rising house prices in the Sydney metropolitan region. On a similar note, the *New Zealand Herald* reported that housing shortages in the country's most populous city – Auckland – were contributing to rising house prices, with around a fifth of the city's suburbs now having average prices in excess of NZ$1 million.

All of these issues are matters of social policy. Social policy issues form the core of most domestic political debates and of some of the major international ones too. Social policies speak directly to the major concerns of our everyday lives: they shape our working lives, school lives and home lives and influence our living standards and living conditions. Social policies address the big questions of who gets what in society, why they should get it and how. It is precisely because social policies deal with these big issues that concern us all that Social Policy is such an interesting and important subject.

Yet, it is also because social policies deal with such big issues that the question of how they might best be studied is open to such debate. Indeed, we can draw a distinction between social policy – a field of government action – and (the capitalised) Social Policy – a field of academic study. In terms of social policy, governments rarely concern themselves with definitional issues of what does or does not constitute a 'social' policy rather than, say, an 'economic' policy: they simply get on with the business of government in whichever way they see fit. In terms of Social Policy, however, there is a need to undertake such definitional work, even if only to determine what ought to be covered by Social Policy textbooks and degree courses. Yet, because social policies cover such wide fields of action and because governments – and social problems – do not stand still, such a task is more difficult than it might appear at first sight. As if this was not enough, academics regularly reassess the core analytic tools and theories that they use to understand issues, and this, in turn, can lead to the boundaries of any subject being redrawn too.

The key pillars of social policy

The long debate among academics about the scope of Social Policy has led to a considerable widening of the subject in recent decades. While this extension of the subject is certainly to be welcomed, our aim here is to provide a *short introduction* to Social Policy. As such, we have taken a deliberate and considered decision to focus on a small number of fields of social policy, omitting discussion of many, very interesting themes in order to make this a concise introduction to the subject. This, of course, raised a question for us as to which areas of social policy to cover in the book and what we offer here is something of a return to 'basics'.

In order to make sense of the complexity of social policy in practice, the main issues of policy are sometimes divided into subjects such as health, housing and employment. In the real world, these fields of policy often overlap, but in most countries, there will be institutional structures – government ministries, civil service departments, administrative offices and research units in universities – that divide reality into these specialist areas. In the traditional language of social policy, these are sometimes referred to as the 'pillars of welfare'. The idea of these issues as 'pillars' goes back to the foundation of the British welfare state in the 1940s, emerging out of the traumatic events of the Second World War. When asked to review some elements of social policy in Britain during this period, the committee led by civil servant William Beveridge published a hugely influential report that provided a blueprint for a new social order in which poverty would become a thing of the past. As the national state was responsible for the war effort, it was to the state that people looked to put these promises into effect afterwards. Looking forward to the reconstruction of Britain after the Second World War, the Beveridge Report (Beveridge, 1942) argued that there were 'five giants' that threatened the well-being of UK citizens in the post-war reconstruction process:

- want (an insufficient income);
- idleness (unemployment through insufficient job opportunities);
- squalor (poor housing conditions);
- ignorance (insufficient or poor-quality education); and
- disease (ill-health exacerbated by insufficient medical assistance).

These five giants map directly onto the five core pillars of welfare we examine in this book (see Table 1.1): social security, employment, housing, education and health. In the aftermath of the Second World War, the British government rapidly expanded and consolidated its activities in each of these areas in order to bring into being what is sometimes regarded as the first example of a 'welfare state' in Britain.

Table 1.1: From Beveridge's five giants to modern-day pillars of welfare

Beveridge's giant	Key issues	Welfare pillar
Want	Insufficient income	Social security
Idleness	Lack of employment opportunities	Employment
Squalor	Poor-quality housing	Housing
Ignorance	Inadequate educational opportunities	Education
Disease	Limited access to health care	Health

As this is an introductory book, we have decided to stick with this orthodox division, partly for simplicity and partly because these institutional structures have, over the years, come to define the reality of modern welfare states. The institutions have taken on a life of their own. These five giants do not, however, cover the entirety of social policy provision. Indeed, other pillars of social policy play an essential role. For instance, it is often argued that there is another central pillar that, broadly speaking, revolves around social care. Some argue that policing and crime prevention are part of the welfare state's pillars too. It might be asked, therefore, why we have chosen to focus on the 'five giants' in this book. In part, the answer is a pragmatic one: in order to deliver a short text, we have, of course, had to omit many themes we find of interest. However, in doing so, we asked ourselves what sorts of issues a student new to the subject would find most useful to see covered in such a book. Our conclusion was that, rather like a tourist guide, a good book should cover the main sights and sounds: while there will always be lots of very interesting sights hidden away from the main boulevards, the first-time visitor needs to grasp the basic layout of a city first in order to orientate themselves in their new location. Our five pillars of welfare represent those main boulevards and each is considered in its own separate chapter. However, we have also added a 'Beyond the five pillars' chapter, which provides a very brief overview of a number of other areas of social policy that stretch beyond the main boulevards covered in more detail.

Analysing social policy: concepts and theories

However, while our focus on the traditional pillars of welfare represents something of a return to basics, we would not be content to merely repeat the time-worn approach to social policy found in the orthodox textbooks. In most of these, each chapter follows its own logic, with rather different social policy themes and issues being discussed under rather different headings. Typically, the author writes from their own national perspective, with a historical overview of policy developments being presented along with a more detailed treatment of the most recent policy developments. In many ways, this makes sense, for the different pillars of social policy do, indeed, deal with quite different social issues. Moreover, in some of the larger texts that deal with policy sectors, theories, ideologies and contextual issues, the sheer diversity of topics makes it difficult to adopt a common structure for each chapter. However, when setting out to write this book, we thought that it ought to be possible in a short text to adopt a more systematic approach that bases each chapter around a common set of theoretically informed themes.

Our approach is based on using a common conceptual framework for each chapter, which helps readers explore the differences and similarities between the 'pillars' and, at the same time, enables comparisons between countries rather than offering an overview of policy developments in just one nation. This allows much greater clarity and enables the real world to be understood and interpreted more easily. Indeed, one of the main problems of the orthodox versions of Social Policy is that they are often somewhat shy about engaging with social theory. We have no hesitation in introducing readers to social theory right at the outset of the book in the belief that this knowledge base is an essential tool, is simply understood and enables a quantum leap for students who can begin very quickly to read both the bigger story of social policy around the planet and to understand their own country and how it fits into the wider picture. Once again, as this is a short introduction to social policy, we cannot offer a comprehensive review of theoretical perspectives and have based our conceptual framework on a favoured piece of work in order to constrain the length of the book.

In his classic text *The three worlds of welfare capitalism*, Esping-Andersen (1990) argued that there are different types of welfare system around the world, with different ideologies and different principles underpinning social policy programmes in different countries. Indeed, as the title of his book suggests, he believed that there were three rather different types of welfare system to be found in the high-income capitalist nations. This was an important observation, for it is sometimes presumed that because social policies are designed to address specific needs that are common to all nations (eg housing policy addresses the universal need for housing), common policy solutions exist around the globe or that a consideration of the evidence will point to a common 'best way' forward. This is far from the case and Esping-Andersen argued that very different responses to common social pressures exist.

Crucially, Esping-Andersen's analysis was not based merely on the analysis of facts and figures or descriptions of the policy systems in each country he analysed. Instead, he drew on rich theoretical debates to help him identify what he suggested were the key features of national welfare systems. Indeed, his book began with a long section on social theory in which he explained his framework for comparing countries: without it, he could make no sense of modern welfare systems and their many differences. On the basis of this review of social theory, he highlighted three key dimensions of social policy on which he felt that differences in approach could be identified across countries.

First, he argued that social policies were concerned with social rights in that they offer individuals protection against the fates that might befall them if they lived in a purely capitalist society in which the only means of generating income was through work. Here, Esping-Andersen built on classic work, such as Marshall's (1950) argument that the development of the welfare state represented the culmination of a long march of rights, providing citizens with important social rights alongside their legal and political rights (for a discussion of social citizenship, see Dwyer, 2010). It has long been observed that social policies are concerned with rights, and the Universal Declaration of Human Rights states that all humans have a right to education and a 'standard of living adequate for their health and well-being' (United Nations General Assembly, 1948: Articles 25 and 26). However, there are many different ways in which these rights can be met and countries vary radically in terms of how extensively they support these social (and human) rights. So, when examining social policies, Esping-Andersen encouraged us to examine the varying strength and nature of these social rights. For instance, in some countries – such as the US – the state only provides healthcare to a minority of people. This means that some people miss out on treatment if they cannot afford it. However, in other countries, such as Sweden, the state provides healthcare to all citizens. While both countries operate healthcare systems for citizens, the extensity of these systems varies radically. Or, in other words, the strength of the social right to healthcare differs.

Building on this question of the nature of social rights, Esping-Andersen argued that varying social rights hinted at broad differences in how societies respond to core social needs. More specifically, he felt that there were key differences in terms of the balance of responsibilities faced by the state, the market, the community and families or individuals. For instance, as in our preceding example, in some societies, the state might play a dominant role in providing healthcare services, but in others, it might be the private market that does so. In other words, Esping-Andersen encouraged us to examine how social policies are organised in different countries. Again, he drew on classic work in the field of Social Policy. Titmuss (1956) famously argued that it was possible to observe a social division of welfare, with welfare being provided not only through state services, but via the tax system and by employers. More recently, theorists have used terms such as welfare pluralism (see Johnson, 1987) or the mixed economy of welfare (see Powell, 2007) to capture the idea that welfare is provided not just by the state, but also by private companies, voluntary organisations and, indeed, families and communities. Esping-Andersen felt that differences between nations in how far they relied on, say, public or private services to meet welfare needs told us a great deal about the nature of their social policies, and he therefore placed this notion of a 'mixed economy of welfare' at the heart of his exploration of social policies.

Finally, and following from the previous two issues, Esping-Andersen suggested that differing social rights and responsibilities had a clear impact on the distribution of resources in societies. For example, a largely privately based system of healthcare might result in richer citizens having better access to services while a state-based system might provide more equal access. Esping-Andersen suggested that all social policies impact on the stratification of society and encouraged us to examine their impact on the distribution of resources and opportunities. Again, he echoed a long tradition of work in the social sciences here, not least classic early pieces of sociology such as Tawney's (1931) *Equality*.

These three issues provide the core themes for each chapter in our book. We have not employed them in strictly the same way as Esping-Andersen did – not least because he only really examined social security in *The three worlds of welfare capitalism* – but they provide the foundation for our approach. Indeed, to simplify matters, we have interpreted the issues in a slightly looser manner, although still following his threefold division of the issues.

First, each chapter of the book begins by asking what the *key policy goals* are that policy might address in each pillar. Thus, the first section of each chapter asks: what might policy aim to do? The crucial point here is that, in practice, policy goals can differ from country to country, so we offer a flavour of the different types of approach that might exist in each sector. Often, these differing policy goals are rooted in different ideologies or different sets of values.

Understanding that policy can have different goals is an important starting point for thinking through how each pillar of welfare might be organised. Indeed, because different countries often try to address different policy goals in each pillar, we often see quite different healthcare, housing and education systems around the world. To demonstrate this, the second section of each chapter explores the *key delivery mechanisms* that might be used in each pillar. It asks: how might services be organised? To echo a point made earlier, it is important to stress that there is no single best approach in each pillar. Instead, there are different policy instruments that have different advantages and disadvantages. In this section of each chapter, we outline the main policy tools along with some of the main pros and cons of each.

This hints at the fact that policy making is often a difficult balancing act: different policy mechanisms will advantage and disadvantage different groups of people and reconciling competing interests is far from easy. The third and final core section of each chapter examines *key policy issues* in each pillar. It asks: who is/is not benefiting from the services delivered in each pillar? In so doing, it aims to examine how policy ameliorates or reinforces social divisions and social inequalities.

Table 1.2 summarises the ways in which Esping-Andersen's framework maps onto ours. While different issues will necessarily be raised in each chapter, each will be organised under the headings in the right-hand column of this table.

Table 1.2: From Esping-Andersen's themes to ours

Esping-Andersen's theme	Key issue	Our headings
Social rights	What is provided	Key policy goals
State, market, family	How it is provided	Key delivery mechanisms
Stratification	Who benefits	Key policy dilemmas

Adopting an international focus

One of the strengths of Esping-Andersen's definition of the core features of social policy is that it can draw attention to different approaches to the provision of welfare in different countries. As well as focusing on the traditional pillars of welfare and examining each through a common set of themes, the third dimension of the approach we have adopted in this book is that it has an international focus. As our book is written in a thematic fashion, we feel that this divorces it from the specifics of a particular national case. As we noted earlier, in most Social Policy textbooks, the individual chapters on health, employment, social security and so on are based around a detailed consideration of practice in the author's own nation. We will instead draw on examples from around the world when exploring the key policy goals, mechanisms and issues in each pillar of welfare.

From an intellectual viewpoint, we feel that the focus on one national case unnecessarily constrains the discussion of social policies: if we are to understand the possibilities of social policy in practice, then it makes sense to reflect on a wider range of national experiences, not least because the differences between nations can often be quite stark. We have tried here to include examples from a very wide range of countries, although data limitations (and, indeed, our own intellectual limitations) mean that there is a bias towards the more heavily researched high-income countries. (The World Bank classifies countries on the basis of their national income per capita [ie per person]. In 2015, countries with a national income of US$12,746 per person or above were classified as being high-income countries.) Crucially, although there are biases towards some countries that we are more familiar with, no single country provides the basis of the discussion in our chapters. Indeed, we draw on evidence and examples from every populated continent of the world, covering over 60 countries in total.

However, we should again stress that our book is merely a short guide; while we will draw on examples from many different countries, we do not aim to provide a comprehensive overview of how nations differ or detailed descriptions of welfare arrangements in different countries. Those readers who wish to gain deeper knowledge of this sort should consult one of the many excellent comparative social policy textbooks that are available.

Concluding remarks

It is hoped that the core features of our approach will now be clear:

- a brief overview of the five core pillars of social policy, each examined individually in their own chapter, with an additional chapter looking 'beyond the five pillars';
- three conceptually rooted themes providing a common structure for each chapter; and
- an international approach that is not rooted in the example of one nation.

In order to meet these goals, we have adopted a particular style of writing that is worth us briefly explaining here.

Each chapter has a relatively short narrative that examines the key issues under our headings of 'key policy goals', 'key delivery mechanisms' and 'key policy issues'. The narrative aims to explain key terms (which are displayed in bold) and to outline the key issues and debates. Examples are kept to a minimum, as are references to other sources. Accompanying the narrative are text boxes and figures that offer greater detail. Sometimes the text boxes and figures offer a case study of one or two nations, sometimes they explore a key debate or concept in more depth, and sometimes they offer useful data or charts. Finally, we draw each of the main chapters to a close by offering a *key points summary* and a *key reading guide*. The latter is particularly important, for we must stress that the aim of this book is merely to provide an *introduction*. To use the guide book analogy once again, while we explore the key features of the main boulevards here, there are so many interesting 'hidden side streets' and 'secret suburbs' that we would encourage you to explore further once you have orientated yourself during your initial visit. Our guide to further reading aims to point you towards the gems of the city that are off the main tourist track described here.

Box 1.1: Interactive content

In this updated second edition of *The short guide to social policy*, we wanted to add value to the first edition published in 2008, but to do so without deviating from our original aim of providing a *brief* introduction to the subject. While we have expanded the printed book a little by extending the original 'Beyond the five pillars' section into a standalone chapter, the main additional content that we have created is not found in the printed book, but in the accompanying app that we have created.

The interactive content works on Apple iOS or Android tablets and smartphones and can be downloaded free of charge; further details, including a guide to use the app, can be found online at http://tinyurl.com/p4wfcur While a number of existing Social Policy textbooks have accompanying websites, ours is the first to have an accompanying app. We have chosen to pursue this route for a number of reasons but chiefly because it allows us to create electronic content that works in harmony with the printed book rather than being a standalone element. Indeed, the app does not function without the book, the interactive content being triggered by scanning QR codes (like the one at the top of this box) printed in the book itself.

Three different types of content can be triggered by scanning these codes, some of which have audio commentary, some of which are text- or graphic-based. They are:

 Short videos with commentary. *Typically, we use these to help interpret the stories behind some of the charts included in the book.*

 Interactive charts. *These are clickable versions of the charts provided in the book that allow you to explore the detail behind a chart in the book (eg to explore more about a particular country in a chart or to see how patterns have evolved over time).*

'Unboxed' boxes. *Each chapter of the book features boxed examples that provide more context on key issues, but these are necessarily limited in their depth by the space available in the book. The 'unboxed boxes' use the abilities of hypertext in order to allow you to explore in more detail key issues raised by some of the boxed examples.*

As the preceding perhaps hints, we have tried to make use of the large amounts of statistical data available on social policy across the world. This is another way in which our book differs from many other introductions to Social Policy. We believe that this kind of data can add hugely to the understanding of social policy, but are equally aware that many readers may view statistics with some degree of trepidation. We hope that our interactive content can help breakdown some of the barriers that students of Social Policy often face in exploring such data.

2

social security

Introduction

Social security is at the heart of the welfare state, but its precise meaning is difficult to pin down, for it often means quite different things in different countries. This is even true of countries that share the same language – such as the UK and US – and reflects the very different historical, political and cultural underpinnings of social policies across the world (see Box 2.1). Given this, the terms 'income protection' or 'social protection' are sometimes preferred to 'social security', for the principal goal of the policies we describe in this chapter is to provide financial support to people whose income is threatened by common events that might, for instance, make it difficult for them to generate sufficient income through paid employment.

The following contingencies, risks and needs are typically covered by 'social security':

- unemployment;
- old age and widow(er)hood;
- sickness;
- disability;
- employment injury and occupational disease;
- raising children; and
- maternity/paternity leave.

A wider definition of 'social security' also includes help with housing costs (see Chapter 6), basic education (see Chapter 4) and a general scheme of financial support for those deemed to have an insufficient income (often called 'social assistance').

The scale and importance of social security schemes can be illustrated by pointing to their costs. In high-income countries, these schemes typically account for between 10% and 20% of gross domestic product (GDP), although countries with the most comprehensive systems sometimes spend as much as 25% of GDP on social security. The sums of money involved are often mind-bogglingly huge as a consequence, typically representing the largest area of government spending in a country. Poorer countries tend to have less comprehensive schemes of support: in low-income countries, social security often accounts for just 1% or 2% of GDP. However, while richer countries tend to spend more, there is no strictly deterministic link between a nation's wealth and the comprehensiveness of its social security system. Indeed, there are places – such as Hong Kong – with high incomes but low spending.

Key policy goals

At the most basic level, the goal of social security can be defined as protecting the income of individuals or families in the face of common contingencies or risks, such as old age or unemployment. To do this, welfare states commonly put in place a series of social security programmes, such as pensions, unemployment benefits, child or family benefits, sickness benefits, and maternity/paternity benefits. In each case, the programme is based primarily around cash transfers from the state to individuals, but sometimes includes benefits-in-kind too (see Box 2.2 later in this chapter).

However, this relatively simple view of social security masks a much more complex set of goals in reality. Income protection may be the core ostensible goal, but there are considerable variations across the developed world in terms of which contingencies are protected against, when they are covered, who is entitled to support and the generosity of the benefit payments. For instance, in the US, a long-term unemployed single man with no dependants would be entitled to very little support from the state; in 2012, such a man who had previously been employed on average wages would have received social security benefits equivalent to a mere 6% of the pay packet that he had previously taken home (OECD, 2014a). By contrast, someone in the same situation in Denmark would have received 58% of his previous salary. Similarly, a man on average earnings who retired in 2013 would have had 63% of his income replaced by the state pension scheme in Finland, but a similar man in the UK would have had just 38% of his income replaced (OECD, 2013).

What these figures indicate is that in making decisions about the seemingly technical issue of 'income protection', governments must also tackle deeply *moral and political questions* about who gets what, when and why. The differences in support for the long-term unemployed in Denmark and the US are stark on paper, and may seem hard to justify, but they reflect differing judgements about how long it is reasonable for the state to support someone without employment who is looking for work. In the short term, the differences in payment levels between these two countries are not so great: 62% and 45% of average earnings are replaced by the schemes in Sweden and the US, respectively (OECD, 2014a). What this demonstrates is that the system in the US is designed around the presumption that an individual may need short-term support when they lose a job, but that after a given period – usually around 20 weeks – they should have been able to find re-employment. The Danish system, however, reflects a quite different view: that structural weaknesses in the economy may sometimes make it difficult for an individual to find appropriate employment. Consequently, their 'short-term' support can last as long as two years and is supplemented by a relatively generous form of longer-term support after this (OECD, 2014a, 2014b). In other words, the two systems differ in terms of how they look to balance a citizen's *rights* to income protection with their *responsibilities* to secure an income through work (see Chapter 3).

Each branch of social security has its own unique policy issues. While a key tension in designing unemployment benefits lies in balancing income protection and stimulating prompt re-entry into the labour market, schemes that supplement the income of those unable to work due to ill-health have to tackle the thorny issue of deciding when someone is too ill to work, and pensions programmes have to make clear when someone is entitled to retire. However, what all social security schemes have in common is that they *redistribute income* within society: from rich to poor, from generation to generation, from those without children to those with children and so on. Given their costs, social security schemes require substantial contributions from taxpayers and businesses in order to finance payments, but how far societies are willing to support the redistribution of income varies considerably.

In his classic study *The three worlds of welfare capitalism*, Esping-Andersen (1990) analysed the protection offered by pensions, unemployment insurance and sickness insurance in 18 developed countries and argued that their welfare states fell into three distinct types, largely on the basis of the strength of their social protections and their redistributional intent:

- *The liberal regime* offers low levels of income protection that often do not stretch beyond providing a basic safety net and little redistribution of income, meaning that the levels of inequality generated by the market largely remain.
- *The social democratic regime* offers high levels of income protection and income is redistributed between social groups with the aim of creating a more equal society.
- *The conservative/corporatist regime* offers high levels of income protection, but there is only a modest redistribution of income between social classes – social security acts as a savings bank to protect against common risks rather than as a tool for promoting greater equality.

In other words, Esping-Andersen found significant differences between countries in terms of policy goals. Crucially, he argued that these variations represented long-term historical differences between nations in terms of the choices that they have made about their social security systems.

Box 2.1: The 'social security' and 'welfare' division in the US

In most countries, the term 'social security' is used to refer to cash transfer programmes as a whole, but in the US, it refers only to the social insurance programmes that exist for older people, disabled people and survivors (widow[er]s). These contribution-based benefits are administered by a federal (ie national) agency – the Social Security Administration – and they operate on an earnings-related basis and make relatively generous payments.

However, the core non-insurance cash transfer programmes are termed 'welfare' and operate on a very different basis. Chief among these is Temporary Assistance for Needy Families (TANF), which is mainly funded by the federal government but is administered by each of the 50 states in the US. The precise details can vary from state to state as a consequence, but the key principles do not: TANF is a means-tested programme that acts as a minimal safety net, paying very modest sums of money to low-income families. In addition, support is very strictly time-limited, with the national rules allowing for no more than five years of support over a person's lifetime. In some states, the maximum period of support is less than this.

The second main plank of 'welfare' in the US comes in the form of the food benefits, formerly known as 'food stamps' but now called the Supplementary Nutrition Assistance Program (SNAP). While social security programmes are mostly based around cash transfers, sometime benefits-in-kind form part of the provision too. Like TANF, SNAP is funded by the federal government but administered by the states. As the old name of 'food stamps' implies, these used to take the form of vouchers or cheques that recipients could use to purchase food. Today, the system is digital, with recipients having credit paid onto an 'Electronic Benefit Transfer' card that can be used to buy approved items from retailers. SNAP forms a substantial part of the welfare package in the US – replacing support that would come as cash in many countries – and the ostensible aim is to promote high levels of nutrition among low-income families.

The separation of social protection into 'social security' and 'welfare' in the US can be seen not just in language, but also in the level and structure of payments, the bodies that administer payments, the length of entitlements, and even the form in which payments are made. All of these factors serve to emphasise the difference between the recipients of the two sets of programmes: while social security recipients are painted as 'deserving' cases, welfare recipients are often portrayed as 'undeserving' and 'welfare dependants', particularly by social conservatives.

These populist divisions play heavily on common stereotypes about which groups are 'hard-working' or 'deserving', which have resonance in many other countries too. In truth, these stereotypes reflect who has the most political power in the US. Lone parents and African-Americans have borne the brunt of welfare reforms since the 1980s because they are disproportionately overrepresented among North America's poor and underrepresented among its political class. Meanwhile, social security – in which middle-class and white North Americans are overrepresented – has seen fewer cutbacks over the same period.

Key delivery mechanisms

The variations that Esping-Andersen (1990) identifies are not just about different levels of spending on particular benefits or different rates of payment to benefit recipients. Just as important are the different delivery mechanisms that are deployed, for while all social security programmes transfer cash payments, the ways in which these payments are organised have a huge impact on the type of support benefit recipients receive. Indeed, the delivery mechanisms that underpin social security programmes often act to institutionalise their core principles.

First and foremost, social security programmes differ in how they determine who is entitled to receive payments. There are essentially three core approaches here: benefits can be universal, means-tested or insurance-based. When benefits are universal, all citizens who meet the relevant contingency receive a payment; in Sweden, for example, a monthly allowance is paid to all families with children irrespective of the household's income (OECD, 2014a). By contrast, a means-tested benefit will only go to those citizens who, when faced with the relevant contingency, are living below a specified income level or without a certain level of assets. In Australia, in 2012, for example, the social assistance safety net targeted at those in severe hardship with no other means of support and no entitlement to other benefits could only be claimed by people with AUS$5,000 or less of available funds or liquid assets (OECD, 2014a). Finally, social insurance benefits are based on the contribution principle: in order to claim a particular benefit when faced with the relevant contingency, a citizen needs to have made a specified number of contributions to the insurance fund. In Germany, for instance, unemployment insurance benefits can only be claimed by those who have made contributions to the fund for at least 12 months in the previous two years – those who do not meet this level have to rely on the less generous social assistance safety net (OECD, 2014a).

In terms of determining benefit payment levels, a distinction is commonly drawn between earnings-related and flat-rate benefits. Earnings-related benefits provide citizens with a cash transfer that equates to a proportion of the income they received from employment before they became sick, unemployed, retired and so on. What this means in practice is that benefit payments will vary from person to person: in Sweden, the initial period of unemployment insurance is paid at 80% of previous earnings (subject to a maximum ceiling), so a woman who had earned SEK600,000 as a doctor would receive higher cash transfers than a man who had worked as a sales assistant with a salary of SEK100,000 per year (OECD, 2014a). When benefits are flat-rate, however, the same level of payment goes to all irrespective of their prior income. This is the case with the unemployment benefit in New Zealand, where in 2012, for example, all single people aged 25 or over were paid NZ$229.01 per week, irrespective of their former income (OECD, 2014a).

Often, it is the case that insurance-based benefits are paid on an earnings-related basis and means-tested benefits are paid on a flat-rate basis. This is because the way in which these benefits are typically financed heavily influences their payment processes. Insurance-based benefits are tied to the contributions made by individuals, often with matching contributions from their employer. As such, benefits of this form can be viewed as social insurance and are not unlike insurance payments that an individual might pay to cover other risks, for example, against their car being damaged in an accident or valuable items being stolen from their home. Social insurance contributions are often fixed as a certain percentage of income – for instance, in 2012, German citizens had to pay 9.8% of their income into pension insurance (OECD, 2013). This means that higher earners pay more into social insurance funds than low earners and it is on this basis that higher payments to higher earners are justified: in principle, there is a direct – actuarial – link between the contributions to a fund and the payments that can be received from it. By contrast, means-tested benefits are typically used when the state wants to target payments at the poorest in society (sometimes means-tested benefits are dubbed 'selective' – as opposed to universal – benefits because of this) and are normally financed through general taxation. Here, entitlement is not based on contribution, but on demonstrated need, and payments are not tied to previous income, but designed to boost incomes that are seen as insufficient. In other words, means-tested benefits tend to have flat-rate, rather than earnings-related, payments. However, it is important to note that this is not always so: there are instances of flat-rate-based social insurance benefits (eg the UK's unemployment insurance benefit – known as Contribution Based Job Seeker's Allowance) and many means-tested benefits offer variable payment levels depending on a claimant's circumstances (eg South Korea has a means-tested social assistance safety net that pays the difference between a household's income and a legally defined minimum cost of living). Moreover, many insurance schemes that appear to be actuarial are, in practice, funded through general taxation, with insurance contributions simply going into the government's coffers rather than into a ring-fenced fund.

In practice, social security programmes almost always involve a mix of the aforementioned benefit types. Indeed, it is common for there to be a more generous insurance-based benefit, which provides cover for insured citizens, supplemented by a less generous means-tested 'safety net' for those who are not insured. Added to this, it is often the case that entitlement to the insurance-based benefit is time-limited – we have already noted that unemployment insurance in the US operates in this way – with claimants having to move to a means-tested benefit after this time. In some countries, even access to the means-tested safety net is time-limited (see Box 2.1). Many countries also stipulate waiting periods before payments are made: in Sweden, for instance, a claim for unemployment insurance is not payable for the first seven days of unemployment. Generally speaking, the rules and restrictions attached to benefits claims tend to be stricter for those deemed able to work; indeed, one of the trends witnessed in recent years has been the increased *conditionality* of payments to those of working age as an attempt to link work and welfare more closely (see Box 2.3 and Chapter 3). This is true both for those who are unemployed – who increasingly have to demonstrate the efforts that they are making to find re-employment – and for those who are sick or disabled – who are being increasingly asked to prove that their condition is severe enough to prevent them from working.

How, then, do the differing *mechanisms* for the delivery of social security relate to the differing *goals* we highlighted earlier? Esping-Andersen (1990) suggested the following:

- The *liberal regime*: strong reliance on means-tested benefits that provide a basic safety net through flat-rate payments.
- The *social democratic regime*: emphasis on generous universal benefits that provide a comprehensive system of social protection.
- The *conservative/corporatist regime*: social insurance benefits predominate, providing a strong system of social protection, but heavy use of earnings-related benefits mutes redistributive impact.

While our emphasis here has been on income protection administered by the state, we should add – following Esping-Andersen again – that the state is far from the only provider of income support (see Box 2.2). In many societies in fact, privately financed and operated schemes – such as pensions or sickness insurance – play a major role. In 2009, in Australia and the US, around one third of pensions-related spending was privately based, and in Canada, almost half was (OECD, 2013). Likewise, 'cash transfers' between family members are hugely significant in many countries, particularly those where family obligations are very firmly culturally embedded. The voluntary sector also plays a role in some countries through organisations such as friendly societies, which organise pooled savings schemes on a not-for-profit basis.

Box 2.2: Income protection beyond the state

The state is by no means the only provider of income protection. In most countries, there are extensive private programmes, particularly in the field of pensions. Indeed, it is very common for pension provisions to be linked to employment in a particular field: so-called 'occupational pensions' that, for instance, might cater for all school teachers in a country. Similarly, in many countries, it is common for individuals to save money in a personal private pension managed by profit-making financial institutions. However, the state usually plays a key role in either encouraging such private programmes (eg through tax breaks on contributions) or discouraging them (eg by providing an extensive public system that negates the need for additional support); its role is rarely neutral. Moreover, it should also be noted that private social spending tends to favour the rich more than the poor, for it caters only for those who can afford to pay into schemes.

In some countries, the not-for-profit sector plays an important role in social security provision. In Sweden, for example, unemployment insurance is administered by a range of unemployment insurance societies that, for the most part, are organised and managed by trade unions, albeit with the state playing a key role in so far as it both endorses the system and makes financial contributions towards it. Religious bodies play a significant role in some countries too. In Italy, for instance, the absence of a national social assistance scheme means that provision is patchy in some regions and/or for some groups, meaning that support provided by churches (mainly benefits-in-kind) have greater significance than in most European countries.

Families play a key role too. While, for most people, families are a natural source of support in times of need, the extent of their role can be heavily influenced by the formal rules of social security systems. For example, in some countries, the income of extended family members may be included in means tests.

Key policy issues

While social security, concerned as it is with applying rules and transferring monies, is a technical and somewhat bureaucratic field of social policy, it should also be clear by now that the rules embedded within social security systems are of enormous significance because of the impact that they have on the strength of social rights, on the distribution of income within society and, more generally, on employment. It is precisely because of this – allied with the huge sums of money involved – that social security can be such a contentious area of policy. Indeed, it is a field where policy makers are faced with some huge policy issues.

If the chief goal of social security programmes is to protect incomes, then we might expect well-functioning systems to eliminate poverty. Yet, the truth is that there is no social security system anywhere in the world that manages to do this completely. Much depends on how we define poverty, an issue over which there is much debate, but Figure 2.1 displays poverty rates in 2010 for the Organisation for Economic Co-operation and Development (OECD) countries using one of the standard poverty measures used in high-income countries: the percentage of individuals living below 50% of median income. It highlights strong variations between countries, with high poverty rates in, for example, the US and Australia (17.4% and 14%, respectively) and more modest levels of poverty in, for example, Denmark and Finland (6% and 7.3%, respectively). Alongside the bars showing the poverty rate in these nations are bars showing the proportion of gross domestic product (GDP) that each country allocates to its core social security programmes: there is, unsurprisingly perhaps, a link between the two, countries with lower poverty rates generally being those with more extensive social security systems. That said, we should note that the link is complex, with other factors such as the state of the economy also having an influence on poverty rates: in Greece and Spain, for example, relatively high social spending and relatively high poverty rates can be found, both countries having seen unemployment and poverty increase significantly following the global financial crisis that began in 2008 (OECD, 2014c).

However, evidence of a link between more extensive social protection and lower poverty rates is not enough to persuade

Figure 2.1: Social security[a] and poverty[b]

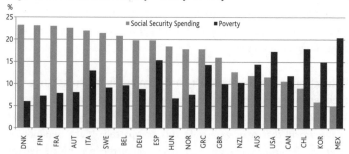

Notes: [a] Public and mandatory private social spending (excluding healthcare), % gross domestic product (GDP), 2010. [b] Percentage of persons living with less than 50% of median equivalised household income, 2010.

Source: OECD.stat.

many decision-makers that an extensive social security system is a necessary investment. As we have hinted throughout, this is in large part a consequence of the substantial level of spending – and therefore taxation – that such a system requires. Added to this are commonplace worries in many countries that increased life expectancy and diminishing birthrates are creating a *demographic time bomb*: fewer future workers to support greater numbers of future pensioners will make systems still more expensive to future taxpayers. Much of the debate about social security in recent years has surrounded the impact that large expenditures have on economic performance. The chief arguments include suggestions that high levels of taxation deter business from investing in the economy and that requiring employers to contribute to social insurance funds makes them less willing to employ people. There is a vocal school of thought which claims that globalisation has heightened these dilemmas because businesses can move their investment from country to country much more easily than in the past. It has also been claimed that generous social security benefits can act as a disincentive to finding work and, consequently, foster 'welfare dependency'. We will explore some of these issues in more detail in Chapter 3.

Box 2.3: Conditionality and sanctions in social security

In recent years, many countries have tightened the conditions attached to receipt of social security benefits for working-age people who are out of work. This increased conditionality entails stipulating behaviours expected from benefit recipients along with sanctions for those who do not comply. For the unemployed, for example, this typically entails requiring claimants to be able to demonstrate that they are actively seeking employment, with the threat that their benefit payments will be reduced or even stopped if they cannot do so. While conditions have long been a feature of social security systems, many analysts suggest that sanctions have become tougher and are being applied more frequently in most countries now.

We deal with the topic of employment in Chapter 4, but as is clear here, social security and employment policies have close connections. Supporters of increased conditionality in social security believe that the use of sanctions can both encourage positive behaviour among benefit recipients and protect the taxpayer against the risk of benefits being claimed unnecessarily. Indeed, the increased conditionality of social security for the unemployed reflects a fear among some policy makers that welfare dependency can occur if unemployment benefits are provided with too few conditions.

However, critics argue that sanctions are disproportionately applied to the least powerful groups in society and that there is scant evidence that sanctions have produced long-term benefits, such as improving employment. Severe sanctions are also likely to cause significant hardship for those affected, potentially leaving them with no form of income from which to meet basic needs. Indeed, some argue that because social security protections are meant to ensure that basic needs are met, conditionality violates social rights.

Although conditionality and sanctions are most commonly used in programmes for the unemployed, there are many examples to be found in other areas of social security. In the OECD, for instance, much attention was gathered internationally by the *Oportunidades* programme in Mexico, which provided cash transfers to low-income families with children on the basis that their children attended school regularly and visited health clinics for check-ups and vaccinations. The idea behind this programme was that boosting the education and health of children from poor families would help break long-term cycles of poverty. Similar conditional cash transfer programmes can be found in a number of middle-income countries and they are particularly common in Latin America.

While there is no clear evidence of a link between strong social protection and weakened economic performance – far from it in fact – many politicians have been keen to at least restrict the growth of social security spending in recent years. Fears among some politicians that social security budgets have expanded to the limits of affordability have, in part, triggered the increased conditionality attached to social rights as governments look to tighten control over spending (see Box 2.3). Another way in which many have tried to limit spending is through greater reliance on means-tested benefits. While the increased targeting that is associated with these benefits can appeal to policy makers keen to get maximum value for money – because cash is focused on the poorest – means-tested benefits carry some inherent problems. Chief among these is the issue of *take-up*. Means-tested benefits typically have lower rates of take-up than universal benefits: many of those who are entitled to claim them do not. There are many reasons for this – including the fact that they are not paid automatically after a particular event (such as retirement), but, instead, have to be actively claimed – but it is often suggested that there is more *stigma* attached to means-tested benefits than to those that are universal or insurance-based. In part, this is because claiming them requires an individual to demonstrate that they are poor by providing a great deal of personal and financial information in order to support their claim. However, on top of this, while universal benefits can be clearly seen as a *social right of citizenship* – because they are paid to all citizens – and entitlement to insurance-based benefits is clearly earned through the payment of contributions, means-tested benefits are often perceived as an '*unearned payment*', '*charity*' or a '*handout*', making some people reluctant to claim them. In some countries, the distinction between means-tested and insurance-based benefits is heavily underlined by the fact that they are administered by separate bodies, institutionalising a commonly held view that there is a division between 'deserving' and 'undeserving' claimants (see Box 2.1).

Another problem that arises with means tests is that of defining the *threshold* against which means are tested. Determining where to draw the line between an income that is deemed sufficient and one that is deemed insufficient is difficult, to say the least. Moreover, in drawing such a line, there is a danger that poverty traps are created when a citizen in receipt of a means-tested benefit can actually see their income drop if increased earnings from employment lead to the withdrawal of their benefits. On top of this, means tests are often assessed against savings and assets, as well as income. In such cases, the aim is to rule out claims from those with substantial amounts of money stored in the bank. While this may seem logical if a benefit is aimed at the poorest, it is often argued that such rules create *perverse incentives* because they penalise those who have saved money for a rainy day. An even thornier issue is that of whose income to assess. Often, it is a family's income that counts rather than simply an individual's, but defining what counts as 'family' can often be a complex task and there are some marked variations across countries. While most equate family with household, there are countries where a family with children making a claim for support will find that the incomes of the children's grandparents and even aunties and uncles will be taken into account when assessing claims for support (see Box 2.2).

Yet, while there are clear problems in utilising means-tested benefits, there are also problems that arise from the heavy use of insurance-based benefits. Chief among these is the fact that they exclude those with a weak contribution record or without one at all because of infrequent or patchy employment. This can be a particular problem for people who have spent considerable periods of time outside of the labour market while caring for family members. As women are more likely to undertake such caring responsibilities in practice, many insurance-based benefits – particularly pension schemes – disadvantage women by failing to account for unpaid work when totting up 'contributions'. While, in principle, universal benefits do not exclude anyone, and should therefore avoid this particular problem, once again, the reality does not always meet the theory. Although universal benefits are paid as a social right of citizenship, most societies contain a not insubstantial number of inhabitants who do not have full citizenship status. In particular, migrant workers and asylum seekers are often denied access to key social security benefits that are ostensibly universal.

It is precisely because access to social security – or the terms on which it is offered – often favours some social groups over others that it is important to look beneath the headline figures on poverty shown in Figure 2.1, for they can mask some of the more subtle social divisions. One of the more prominent trends in high-income countries is that the rates of poverty are much higher for lone-parent households than for couple households with children, as shown in Figure 2.2. Again, however, there are important differences between countries. Some work hard to reduce poverty in single-parent households through the social security system. For instance, in 2012, Denmark paid all lone parents DKK5,200 per year on top of normal family allowances and another DKK5,104 per child per year too – and more still if the absent parent did not make any contributions to household income (OECD, 2014a). Other nations, however, often penalise lone-parent households,

Figure 2.2: Poverty[a] and family type

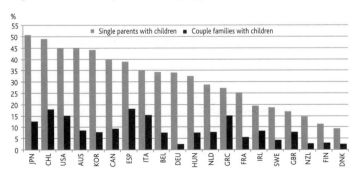

Note: [a] Households living on less than 50% of median income, 2010.

Source: OECD.stat.

either by providing very low rates of support or, in some cases, by favouring married couples in the taxation system. Social security is not the only factor influencing these different outcomes however, varying patterns of employment have an influence (see Chapter 3), as well as the affordability and accessibility of childcare (see Chapter 7).

What all this suggests is that far from being 'merely' concerned with protecting incomes, social security rules are heavily shaped by power relations in society. While it is beyond the scope of this book to explore this issue, we might reflect on it by noting that despite displaying the highest levels of poverty in most developed societies, lone-parent households are one of the groups that has been most consistently targeted by politicians looking to restrict social security entitlements in recent years. Another group is the unemployed. By contrast, politicians often look on payments towards pensioners more favourably. This, in turn, hints at another important feature of social security systems that is often overlooked: they are well used by the *rich as well as the poor*. While it is often presumed that the bulk of social security spending goes to the poorest or most marginalised groups in society, this is not the case in practice. Indeed, most social spending in rich countries is allocated to pensions and healthcare (OECD, 2014d: 177), areas of spending that are widely drawn on by all income groups. A detailed study undertaken in the mid-2000s suggested that, across OECD countries, the poorest 30% of working-age households received only a marginally greater share of income transfers than the richest 30% in Germany and France, while in Italy and Portugal, the richest 30% actually received more than twice as much as the poorest 30% (Förster and d'Ercole, 2005).

KEY POINTS SUMMARY

- Social security is concerned with providing income protection.
- Social security guards against common risks and contingencies, such as unemployment and old age.
- It does this primarily through cash transfers.

- Social security takes many different forms, including means-tested, universal and insurance-based benefits.
- Payment rates vary substantially and can be earnings-related or flat-rate.
- Social security has a huge impact on poverty and inequality in societies.
- Social security is usually viewed as a government activity, but the private and voluntary sectors play a key role too, as do families.
- Social security caters for the rich and poor.
- Social security embodies deeply moralistic principles.

KEY READING GUIDE

Good overviews of social security can be found in most core Social Policy textbooks. Particularly useful examples include: the chapter by McKay and Rowlingson (2012) in Alcock et al's *The student's companion to social policy*; chapter five of *Understanding social policy* by Hill and Irving (2009); Fitzpatrick's (2012) chapter on 'Cash transfers' in Baldock et al's *Social policy*. More detailed and specialised accounts can be found in Millar's (2009) *Understanding social security* and Spicker's (2011) *How social security works*. Shildrick et al's (2012) *Poverty and insecurity. Life in low-pay, no-pay Britain* challenges some of the myths surrounding work, unemployment, poverty and the welfare state.

The OECD provides a lot of easily accessible information about social protection arrangements in the high-income countries on its website at www.oecd.org. Two particularly useful publications it issues are *Benefits and wages* (OECD, 2014a, 2014b) and *Society at a glance* (OECD, 2014d). Those interested in a more detailed account of national features of social security should also consider the US Social Security Administration's webpage on 'Social security programs throughout the world' (available at: www.ssa.gov/policy/docs/progdesc/ssptw/), which provides concise information on coverage, qualifying conditions and benefit levels, as well as the financing of the main social security programmes in 170 countries all over the world.

3

employment

Introduction

In Chapter 2, we stressed that the precise definition and classification of social security schemes is a difficult endeavour. This is certainly true for employment policies too. A *narrow* definition of the term typically separates so-called passive or reactive labour market programmes from active ones. Simply put, passive programmes look to provide income protection (see Chapter 2) for those without work, while active programmes aim to help those without work to find (re-)employment. The most common example of a passive employment policy is the payment of unemployment benefit. As we will discuss in this chapter, such policies have come to be viewed in an increasingly negative light, with many arguing that they are detrimental to the cause of solving the most severe labour market problems.

The Organisation for Economic Co-operation and Development (OECD) identifies five main types of active employment programmes (Adema et al, 2011):

■ First, there are *employment services*. While the precise nature of these services varies from country to country, public employment agencies or job centres are typically responsible for placing the unemployed into the labour market by matching them with job vacancies and providing advice on work opportunities. They often also administer payments of unemployment benefits and allocate jobless persons to available slots in other labour market programmes such as training schemes.

- Second, *labour market training* can be offered to the unemployed in the form of vocational training or academic training, and it is sometimes offered to the already employed to help ensure their future employability in changing labour markets.
- Third, in many countries, there are specific *youth programmes* that either target young unemployed people or offer apprenticeships or craft training for young school leavers.
- Sometimes, these tie in with a fourth approach, which is *subsidised employment*. In some countries, subsidies are paid to private sector companies in order to encourage the hiring of unemployed people. Typically, these schemes contribute to a firm's wage costs if they agree to employ someone who has been out of work for a long period of time. Sometimes, these subsidies can also be paid directly to the unemployed by granting financial support if they wish to start their own business. Furthermore, governments can also create jobs directly in the public sector or in non-profit organisations.
- Fifth, the OECD also points to specific *measures for disabled people*. Albeit that this is a somewhat crude classification, it is intended to highlight the special vocational training programmes and sheltered employment programmes that many countries use to increase the employment rates of disabled people.

On average, spending for all of the aforementioned active labour market programmes accounted for 0.6% of gross domestic product (GDP) across the OECD in 2011, with the highest spenders in the OECD allocating between 1.0% and 2.2% of their GDP on activation policies, while the lowest spenders merely reached between 0.1% and 0.2% of GDP (see Table 3.1).

Another way to look at the scale and importance of active labour market programmes is to relate them to expenditure on passive unemployment benefit payments. Only a few OECD countries, namely, Norway, Sweden and Poland, spend more on active than on passive labour market measures (see also Table 3.1). Most countries spend around twice as much on unemployment benefits as they do on active labour market programmes.

Table 3.1: Active labour market and unemployment benefit spending

	ALMP spending (% GDP)	Unemployment benefit spending (% GDP)	ALMP spending as % of unemployment benefit spending
Denmark	2.2	2.2	100
Sweden	1.2	0.4	300
Netherlands	1.1	1.5	73.3
Finland	1.0	1.7	58.8
France	0.9	1.6	56.3
Spain	0.9	3.5	25.7
Austria	0.8	0.9	88.9
Germany	0.8	1.2	66.7
Norway	0.6	0.4	150
Portugal	0.6	1.2	50
Switzerland	0.6	0.6	100
Hungary	0.4	0.8	50
Poland	0.4	0.2	200
United Kingdom	0.4	0.4	100
Czech Republic	0.3	0.7	42.9
Korea	0.3	0.3	100
New Zealand	0.3	0.4	75
Canada	0.2	0.7	28.6
Japan	0.2	0.3	66.7
United States	0.1	0.8	12.5

Notes: ALMP = active labour market programme; GDP = gross domestic product; 2011

Source: OECD.Stat.

This *narrow* definition of employment policy as a trade-off between active and passive labour market measures is not uncontested. To begin with, its focus on *public* employment services – that is, those operated by the state – disregards private sector activity. In some countries, privately operated recruitment agencies actually play a larger role than those operated by the state. Similarly, private businesses operate forms of job training and apprenticeships that are important in many countries but are not taken account of in the OECD figures.

More importantly, however, the activation of unemployed persons or income protection against the contingency of joblessness is only part of the many ways in which states can and do influence the functioning of national economies and labour markets. It is common sense that unemployment is dependent on the overall economic situation. As a consequence, sound economic policies that promote economic growth and stability are often seen as the most effective employment policies (see Chapter 7). Interestingly, while empirical research seems to verify the negative link between unemployment and economic performance, the fundamental question about how best to encourage growth is a far from technical one. All around the world, policy makers, professionals and academics still engage in heated political debates on this important issue (see Box 3.1).

In addition, several other dimensions of social policy also have an influence on employment levels. In particular, *education* and *immigration policies* have to be mentioned at this point as they influence not only the number of people seeking employment, but also the skills base of national labour forces (see also Chapter 4). *Family policies* often determine how much parents struggle to reconcile working careers and family life as the provision of childcare, in particular, has a positive effect on overall employment rates. *Labour market regulations* such as mechanisms for wage-setting and rules relating to employment contracts – determining, for instance, the number of working hours, holidays or the membership and density of union membership and work councils across industries – also have an impact on both employers' and employees' work and employment decisions.

A thorough account of employment policies cannot be content with merely differentiating between passive and active policy measures alone, but must take note of all of the aforementioned mechanisms.

Box 3.1: Unemployment – which unemployment?

According to the standard International Labour Organisation (ILO) definition, 'unemployment' refers to persons who are without work, are available for work and are actively seeking work (see: www.ilo.org). The unemployment rate, which is most commonly reported in media coverage around the globe, refers to the share of unemployed persons of the so-called labour force. This labour force is itself calculated as the sum of all persons employed and unemployed.

While international organisations like the ILO have made great progress in standardising unemployment rates, many countries still use registered unemployment figures for official statements – they simply count how many unemployed persons claim unemployment-related benefits at any given time. While such data is much easier to obtain than self-reported unemployment based on large-scale household panel surveys, it is severely flawed as it excludes all those unemployed persons who are not entitled to, or choose not to claim, such benefits. For example, registered unemployment figures do not contain those unemployed persons receiving income support or other forms of social assistance. As barriers to claiming unemployment-related benefits vary substantially across different nations (see Chapter 2), registered unemployment figures are not comparable.

Full employment has been the manifested goal of many governments around the world. However, full employment should not be understood as a situation in which the unemployment rate is 0%. Instead, frictional unemployment counts people who are between two different jobs. For example, if a constructer's contracted work is finished, it may take some time for him/her to find another assignment. It is widely accepted that this form of unemployment is not very problematic and will always persist even in nations with extraordinarily strong economies.

Structural unemployment is caused by fundamental change in the demand for certain workers and skills. Jobs can become obsolete if economies change their operations. For example, the use of more efficient machinery has been one of the main causes of both productivity growth and the elimination of labour in the agriculture and manufacturing sectors. In a globalised world, competitor nations might simply be able to produce certain goods at lower prices, resulting in the relocation of economic activity to these countries. For example, large parts of textile industries have moved out of the relatively 'expensive' high-income countries since the mid-1970s. The mass-scale introduction of computers – combined with a series of mergers of transnational corporations in order to reduce administrative costs – has led to layoffs of thousands of employees in banking and other service sectors across the world. Attempts to contain government budgets in order to keep taxation low have led to substantial reductions in the number of public employees in many countries too.

Structural changes of the economy are among the main reasons for prolonged spells of unemployment today. Definitions of long-term unemployment differ, but they typically refer to unemployment spells longer than 12 or even 24 months. The real danger for workers is not having to find identical work for another employer after a brief spell of unemployment (as in the case of frictional unemployment), but losing employment in a particular branch of the economy and being forced to find employment in a branch that requires very different skills. It is these forced career changes that are most regularly associated with long-term unemployment, which, in turn, poses a real poverty risk. The long-term unemployed are the prime recipients of most of the different demand- and supply-side policy measures discussed in this chapter.

Key policy goals

Unemployment is among the main causes of poverty, social exclusion and social inequality. It is often related to serious personal and social problems, such as stress, low self-esteem, marital breakdown and ill-health. The seriousness of unemployment increases with its duration, while the length of unemployment spells is itself among the most important determinants of individuals' employment prospects. The 'employability' of excluded individuals from the labour market decreases substantially with time.

For governments, unemployment tends to inflate budget deficits as spending for passive and active unemployment measures rises automatically with the number of recipients. At the same time, increases in unemployment can lead to reductions in tax revenues as jobless persons are often exempt from paying income tax, national insurance contributions and sometimes even VAT. As a consequence, governments may be forced to increase taxes and contributions for the working population or to cut government spending for education, healthcare or infrastructure.

The aim of boosting labour market participation rates – that is, the aim of getting as many persons into paid employment as possible – has been at the heart of attempts to alleviate social disadvantages and to promote social inclusion. Added to this, demographic changes in many countries mean that dependency ratios (the ratio of children and pensioners to persons of working age) are projected to grow substantially in the course of the next 20 to 30 years, making the increase of employment rates a necessity if existing welfare state arrangements are to be financed without very significant tax rises.

In recent years, traditional social security or income protection schemes have increasingly been under attack for being detrimental to the goal of boosting labour market participation rates. It has been argued that what we have called passive benefits effectively reduce the labour supply, which, in turn, leads to slower economic growth, higher structural unemployment and eventually further strains on state budgets. For example, it is claimed that unemployed individuals who receive too generous unemployment benefits have an incentive to delay their return to work. Rather than encouraging jobless persons to seek paid employment, passive social security or income protection is seen by some as the cause of a dependency culture. Terms like 'unemployment traps' or 'poverty traps' are often mentioned in connection with these arguments. Consequently, policy makers in many different countries have promoted activation as the dominant goal of employment policies.

In reality, employment rates differ substantially from country to country. Data on labour market participation is not available for all countries around the world, but ILO estimates suggest that the share of employed and self-employed people as a proportion of the total working-age population does not usually exceed the 80% mark. Most of the countries in Figure 3.1 reached employment rates of between

Figure 3.1: Total employment^a

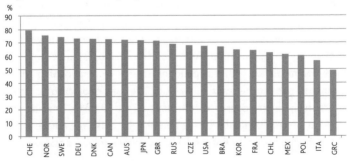

Note: ^a As a percentage of the working-age population (15–64), 2013.

Source: OECD.stat.

60% and just over 75% in 2013. There are some countries with rates of only around or even well below 50%. This tells us that despite the aim to bring as many people as possible into paid employment, there is still significant room for improvement in most countries.

We should not, however, overemphasise the issue of the quantity of work in promoting well-being, for the *quality* of work is equally important here. High levels of employment and economic progress are not sufficient if workers are restricted from sharing in the wealth that they helped to create. For example, the ILO has fought to make freedom of association (ie the right to join a trade union) and the elimination of compulsory and child labour, as well as the elimination of gender, religious and racial discrimination at the workplace, a reality. A majority of countries around the globe have committed themselves to different ILO conventions since its creation in 1919. While the ILO has achieved its goals for many workers, it is still a long way short of doing so for all workers across the world.

Inside the European Union (EU), the European Social Charter requires member states to adopt policies to guarantee non-discriminatory remuneration, a minimum working age of 16 years, maximum hours of work per week, minimum health and social security provision (including minimum pension rights), and free association in trades unions and collective bargaining (for more information, see: www.coe.int/t/dghl/monitoring/socialcharter/). The proposal of the Social Charter triggered serious disputes among the EU member countries at first and only with some delay did all EU member states eventually agree to sign it. These provisions go beyond those in the ILO conventions, highlighting key issues about workplace safety and even remuneration that fall under the umbrella of employment policy. In some countries, the state plays a significant role in regulating labour market pay in an effort to ensure that work delivers a living wage. Some also regulate contracts to guard against the easy dismissal of employees in order to promote the greater stability of employment.

These examples illustrate that there are significant variations across countries in terms of the specific tools used to expand employment rates and in terms of what is understood as the most favourable level of income and employment protection for employees. The illustration of different replacement rates for long-term unemployed people in Chapter 2 gave a first indication of this. We will now expand on this in more detail.

Key delivery mechanisms

The ways in which countries try to maintain high levels of employment are manifold. To make some sense of the various policy tools at the disposal of state governments, the literature broadly distinguishes between so-called demand- and supply-side policy instruments that can be used to influence national labour markets. According to this view unemployment occurs if there is an imbalance between the supply of labour (ie the number of people seeking work) and the demand for labour (ie the number of jobs on offer from employers). Supply-side policies aim to increase the number of people (or, more specifically, the number of people with the necessary skills) looking for work, while demand-side policies aim to create the economic conditions that will lead employers to need more workers.

Communist-style socialist economic planning has offered the most direct and radical approach to managing the demand side of the labour market. For instance, at the height of its socialist planning system, the government's labour bureaux allocated all jobs in China. Jobs were guaranteed for life and wages were determined by the state. Since the late 1970s, the Chinese system has been significantly reformed, but the state (not least through state-owned enterprises) is still at the heart of the economy. Although this is an extreme example, it is worth noting that, historically at least, capitalist economies have also engaged heavily in direct job creation as a means of sustaining high employment levels. Indeed, a central plank of so-called Keynesian economics is the notion that states could smooth out peaks and troughs in demand by injecting public money into the economy when unemployment is rising. In many countries, the post-war years saw an expansion of state ownership in the economy as a consequence; in the UK, for instance, the state once owned and controlled many key businesses in the fields of transport, motor vehicle production, telecommunications and energy production. Employees in these state-owned industries were, to a degree, insulated from downward swings in the economy because the state could use public money to cover shortfalls in income and so avoid the need for job losses. Indeed, many of these industries were, in fact, initially nationalised (ie moved from private hands into state ownership) in order to protect against job losses that would have otherwise occurred.

While programmes of nationalisation have lost some of their attractiveness since the 1980s – many economists argued that they led to the state subsidising inefficient businesses or unpopular products and, as a consequence, many nationalisations were reversed through programmes of privatisation – examples of Keynesian-type labour market programmes can still be found, although the investment tends to be in areas of the economy that are less likely to be seen as part of the private sector's domain. A good example of such an initiative is South Africa's Expanded Public Works Programme (EPWP), which was formally launched in the year 2004 and is still being implemented (see: www.epwp.gov.za/). This government initiative initially aimed to create up to 750,000 jobs by investing in the construction and improvement of existing roads, water drains and urban pavements, as well as a further 300,000 jobs through various environmental projects, between 2004 and 2009. This public works programme echoes one of the most famous early attempts to use the state's spending power to combat unemployment: the US's New Deal programme that was implemented as a response to the Great Depression of the 1930s.

It should also be noted that most countries directly employ considerable numbers of people in public services such as health and education, which are at the core of the welfare state, and as members of the civil service, judicial system and police and armed forces. Through its control of these services, the state is more often than not the biggest single employer in a country and any attempt to expand or contract public services can have an important impact on employment levels. Indeed, in the 1980s and early 1990s, Sweden used the expansion of its welfare services as both a tool for guarding against rising unemployment during a major recession of the world economy and as a strategy for increasing the participation rate of women in the labour market. Contrarily, the introduction of arguably more efficient and cost-effective New Public Management methods in Germany led to many public sector workers being made redundant during the 1990s and early 2000s. While this was dubbed a necessary step to modernise public services in Germany, it undoubtedly aggravated the already tense situation in the German labour market during those years.

Finally, governments often aim to influence demand via fiscal policy. While the large-scale nationalisation of businesses is off the cards politically in many nations, some governments still resort to Keynesian-inspired demand management ideas by looking to reduce taxation during times of low demand. Crudely put, the aim here is to inject extra money into the economy via tax cuts in the hope that people will spend this money and so, in turn, help reinvigorate the economy. The downside of cutting taxation is that governments have to then borrow money to cover the spending that taxes would have covered. In classic Keynesian thought, these budget deficits would need to be recovered by increased taxes once the economy is in better health.

As we have hinted earlier, there has been a significant shift in thinking in recent decades that has taken governments away from demand management techniques. Although some governments did turn back to these demand-side approaches to a degree during the global financial crisis (see Box 2.3), employment policies have increasingly focused on supply-side measures and, in particular, active labour market policies (ALMPs). This shift has not been without its critics, many of whom have seen it as a process of weakening citizens' social rights and increasing their obligations.

It is not hard to see why some people have made this case. Historically, the first forms of social insurance in the pioneer welfare states granted compensation for workers and their families in cases of occupational disease and work injury, thus indicating a sense of responsibility on the states' or employers' side in cases in which workers lose the ability to gain a labour market income through no fault of their own. The subsequent – and often quite significantly delayed – implementation of unemployment benefit systems has to be seen in the light of a growing understanding of the existence of economic cycles and the notion that markets may simply not create enough of the demanded employment at times. The relative generosity of unemployment benefits in countries such as Sweden has sometimes been explained as a kind of state insurance against the insecurity of world markets.

Much of the thrust of the activation agenda goes against this grain because it attempts to make the payment of unemployment benefits *conditional* on the citizen's participation in schemes that will make them more employable (see Chapter 2). For instance, in many countries, the receipt of benefit is now only available to the long-term unemployed if they agree to participate in academic education, accept labour market training or subsidised employment, take work experience, or do community work. In some countries, citizens may have their benefit withdrawn if they refuse to accept a job that the state deems suitable even if the citizen is qualified to work in a quite different field.

Thereby, the increased conditionality of benefits can be seen as part of a broader set of strategies that aim to make work pay by reducing the overall generosity of support for the unemployed, and in many countries, the levels of unemployment benefit payments have also been reduced as part of this process. Rather than stressing the cyclical nature of the economy and the need for social protection against economic downturns, the thrust of these reforms has been to stress the responsibility of individuals to find work and – as already mentioned earlier – the risks of generous benefits reducing incentives for individuals to find work.

Another set of supply-side policies that have become popular with governments in recent years has focused around attempts to increase the flexibility of labour markets. The question of employment protection is an important one. Similar to the critique of passive social security measures, rigid labour markets have been attacked for creating barriers for employment as, for example, they are said to limit the speed with which businesses can respond to short-term increases or decreases in work orders.

Yet, the stringent regulation of hiring and firing is but one feature of a rigid labour market. In some countries, employers' associations have argued that permissible hours of work are too tightly regulated and compensation for overtime work is too generous to enable businesses to adjust their production to short-term changes in the demand for goods. It has also been argued that powerful trades unions can prevent flexibility by protecting incumbent workers to the detriment of labour market outsiders more generally. Others have stressed that the costs of employers contributing to the healthcare and pensions expenses of their employees can act as a disincentive to them employing extra workers, particularly if the global market allows them to shift production to countries where there are fewer requirements to make such contributions. As a consequence of all this, some countries have looked to water down employment protections in the belief that a less rigid labour market will remove barriers to employment growth by attracting international investments.

However, it would be wrong to suggest that supply-side activation strategies are all about increasing obligations and reducing rights. In reality, ALMPs typically feature a mix of so-called 'carrots and sticks'. For example, *make work pay* strategies are not exclusively about increasing the conditionality of unemployment benefits. Many governments have also tried to encourage the employment of long-term unemployed people by reducing the costs for employers of hiring persons in the low-wage labour sector. Governments can do this not only by granting subsidies to employers to hire the long-term unemployed, as mentioned earlier, but also by decreasing non-wage labour costs (eg by shifting the financing of income protection systems away from employers' social contributions to general taxation). In addition, many governments have increased the use of in-work benefits by, for example, topping up low-wage workers' income through tax credits in an attempt to remove the poverty traps that many benefit claimants face (see Chapter 2). On a similar note, national minimum wage schemes are designed to raise the disposable incomes of workers with low earnings. Discussions about the introduction of a 'living wage' calculated according to the basic cost of living in a given country have been more prominent in recent years (see: www.livingwage.org.uk/).

Improved family policies have also been identified as a crucial strategy for increasing employment rates as they make it easier for parents – particularly for women – to reconcile family life and working careers (see Chapter 7). Empirical evidence suggests a clear link between policy measures such as free basic education for children, the existence of all-day schools, generous maternity leave schemes and good childcare, on the one hand, and the number of women joining the labour force, on the other. Some nations have, therefore, looked to considerably strengthen policies in these areas as part of their efforts to boost employment rates.

Box 3.2: The US response to the global financial crisis

Originating in the collapse of the US mortgage market (see Chapter 6), the 2008 global financial crisis had a huge impact on the country. By 2009, the number of homes facing foreclosures because their owners were no longer able to repay their mortgages rose to 2.8 million (a 120% increase compared to 2007). US GDP contracted by 2.4% during the same year (the largest annual decline of GDP in real terms on record in the post-war era), while unemployment peaked at 10% (rising from a comparatively low 4.6% in 2006). The increase of the US federal budget deficit – from US$455 billion to US$1.4 trillion during 2008–09 – was unprecedented in US post-war history (Béland and Wadden, 2011).

The US government responded by enacting a mix of fiscal and employment policies aimed at re-establishing trust in the US banking sector, investing in jobs and infrastructure and strengthening income protection schemes to support workers and the ailing US economy. First, the US treasury was permitted to buy US$700 billion troubled mortgage-based assets through the so-called Emergency Economic Stabilisation Act of 2008 (sometimes refered to as the Troubled Asset Relief Programme [TARP]). The same programme was later used to support the US automotive industry in order to prevent workers from losing their jobs.

Second, in 2009, the American Recovery and Reinvestment Act included both passive and active labour market programmes in an attempt to support the US labour market more directly. Active labour market measures included an extension of employment services and training availability, a series of subsidised employment measures, and an extension of the duration and benefit levels of unemployment insurance. These changes went hand-in-hand with a series of improvements of the US social safety net: food-based, community-based and immunisation programmes were extended, while many Americans received a one-off payment of US$250. A public works programme intended to create 1.25 million jobs through direct public infrastructure investment was undertaken, while those who lost their jobs as a consequence of the crisis could make use of a temporary health insurance programme. Together with substantial expenditure on tax breaks for individuals and businesses and direct aid to states, the American Recovery and Reinvestment Programme was by far the largest economic stimulus package enacted anywhere in the world as, in absolute terms, these different measures added up to a total of $US787 billion in additional spending (ISSA, 2010).

Most commentators judge the US government's crisis response positively. Indeed, while the social and economic consequences of the crisis are still being sharply felt by many Americans, the main economic indicators have outperformed those of other high-income economies and are estimated to do so for at least another few years: annual GDP growth in 2014 was 2.3% compared to 1.3% for the OECD as a whole; and the US unemployment rate fell from its peak in 2009 and is projected to reach almost pre-crisis level by 2016 – in comparison, the unemployment rate for other OECD countries is projected to stubbornly remain at around 7% (OECD, 2014e).

The vast investment in the US economic recovery has thereby not led to any major increase in consumer prices, while the US fiscal balance has reduced at a faster rate than in many other countries that put a bigger emphasis on deficit reduction by freezing public expenditures in response to the crisis (IMF, 2012).

Key policy issues

What are, perhaps, the core dilemmas in employment policy are no doubt implicit in the preceding discussion: there is often a tension (or a perceived tension) between measures designed to promote the quantity of jobs and those designed to improve the quality of jobs. Similarly, there is also a tension between efforts to protect citizens against the risks of unemployment and the risk that those protections may harm efforts to promote re-employment.

Indeed, the main rationale behind the growing emphasis on activation policies in many countries is that generous social security benefits are thought by some to reduce the supply of labour, which is at odds with the principal goal of employment policies to maintain and increase high levels of employment. Similar to the notion of the so-called poverty trap (see Chapter 2), some analysts have argued that income protection schemes can produce unemployment traps, which foster a culture of welfare dependency. Let us return to our example of differences in benefit generosity for the long-term unemployed introduced in Chapter 2: we might ask whether or not it is plausible to suggest that a long-term unemployed person in Denmark who receives 58% of their previous salary should be more inclined to remain out of paid employment for longer (eg in order to wait for the right job that fits their qualifications and is reasonably close to their home) than a long-term unemployed person in the US who can only expect 6% of their previous income. Is it not self-evident that an unemployed person receiving 58% of their previous salary should be much better able to maintain their living standard, while an unemployed with 6% of their previous income will feel much more pressure in that sense?

Certainly, many policy makers seem to think that there are good reasons for making such claims, but the evidence is far from clear-cut. The comparison of net unemployment benefit replacement rates (a commonly used indicator to measure the generosity of unemployment benefit systems) with incidences of long-term unemployment caution us against jumping to rash conclusions (see Figure 3.2). Several countries in the OECD with the highest net benefit replacement rates for unemployment (eg Denmark, Finland and Austria) do not suffer from excessive long-term unemployment in relative terms. Similarly, some countries with the highest share of long-term unemployed people among the jobless only show average or even very low net benefit replacement rates for unemployment. Long-term unemployment has been a serious issue in Greece and Italy although these countries have among the least generous unemployment benefit systems among the countries presented in Figure 3.2; Norway – the country with the lowest rate of long-term unemployment in the OECD (apart from South Korea) – is commonly seen as having one of the most generous social security systems worldwide. Unfortunately, similar data is still hard to come by for countries outside the OECD, but we have no reason to believe that such automaticity between unemployment benefit generosity and long-term unemployment actually exists in the middle- and low-income countries.

At the same time, it would be wrong to suggest that unemployment traps are not a real issue in many countries. The fact that disposable income can potentially drop with the acceptance of employment in the low-income sector is a reality for many unemployed people. Moreover, there is some evidence suggesting that placement efforts, increased obligations and conditionality can help to bring unemployed people back into work faster. The statistics presented in Figure 3.2 merely intend to suggest that while supply-side activation policies undoubtedly have some positive effects, they should not be seen as a panacea to the problems in contemporary labour markets.

Indeed, one major limitation of active labour market programmes is that they only work if the increased supply of labour they create matches demand in the labour market. Supply-side activation policies do not

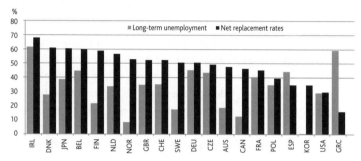

Figure 3.2: Net replacement rates[a] and long-term unemployment[b]

Notes: [a] Average over the 60 months of benefit receipt, including housing benefits and social assistance, 2011. [b] Percentage of unemployed out-of-work for one year and over, 2012.

Source: OECD.stat.

create jobs by themselves. A particular issue here is that structural changes in national economies often lead to the dismissal of workers whose specific skills have lost their value in the labour market. This has happened in many high-income countries as a by-product of the transformation from manufacturing-based industrial economies to service-based, knowledge economies. Processes of deindustrialisation pose real challenges for employment policy. The closure of an industry that provided employment for a large number of workers in an area can be devastating for a whole city or region and activation policies can do little when there are thousands of workers with unwanted skills all looking for re-employment in the same place at the same time. For such workers – many of whom might well be in their 40s or 50s and look back at long working careers – cutbacks in benefits and increased conditionality will have an uncertain impact on their employment prospects but will almost certainly increase their risk of falling into poverty.

Mismatches in the skills level of national labour forces and the demand in national economies have increasingly become a reality in many countries. Policy makers are facing the paradox that long-term unemployment often persists at relatively high levels, while employers complain that they cannot find sufficiently skilled personnel to staff job vacancies. One possible route for governments out of this dilemma has been to increase efforts to attract highly skilled workers from foreign countries – a strategy that has often been instrumentalised by populist parties. Skills shortages are becoming a more and more important issue in emerging economies around the world too. The pattern is very similar: although countries like China and India have comparably large labour forces at their disposal, foreign companies have warned that they often cannot find Chinese or Indian nationals with the skills and qualifications that are in demand. Hence, developing more comprehensive education systems has become a top priority in these countries (see also Chapter 4).

Despite the problems of deindustrialisation that most high-income countries have faced, their overall employment rates have generally witnessed an upward trend. In particular, increases in female labour market participation have been formidable since the 1960s. However, many of the newly created jobs in these countries are less secure than the ones that they have replaced: many are temporary and part-time, or jobholders are subject to slimmer chances of being promoted over the years. While this is not necessarily a negative development – job-splitting and sharing initiatives have gained attention in recent years – it has been suggested that a shift towards a more knowledge-based economy has produced a growing divide between those with high skills who are more likely to be in well-paid and secure jobs and those with low skills who are more likely to be in low-paid and insecure jobs. Certainly, it is the case that income inequality has increased in many countries as the labour market has changed and that the only chance for many long-term unemployed and low-skilled youths to find employment is often in the low-income sector. It is also the case that in the emerging knowledge economies, the risk of becoming unemployed – and of remaining in unemployment for a long period – is strongly associated with educational and professional qualifications.

It is partly because of this that many states have begun to stress the importance of *investment in human capital* (ie the education and training of individuals) as both an economic and social strategy: in other words, equitable access to quality education and training from an early age is key for future working careers. Indeed, more and more policy makers suggest that this is a route to squaring the often competing objectives of social and economic policy, although such arguments have fierce critics.

One of the main criticisms of this thinking is that it may do more to help those with strong skills and high levels of education than it helps those without. Indeed, people who work in the growing low-income sector can often find that their wages alone are not sufficient to lift them out of poverty; this is particularly so if – as is happening in some countries – the financial rewards going to those in high-skill occupations are increasing at a much faster rate than the rewards for those in lower-skill occupations. In fact, some countries have experienced a growing number of 'working poor'.

While the introduction of a national minimum wage is seen as an important tool to help alleviate this problem, the question of what level of income is perceived as a sufficient minimum is important here. About three quarters of EU member states had some form of statutory national minimum wage in 2013 (see Table 3.2), but the rates varied from merely €157.5 per month in Romania to €1,874.2 per month in Luxembourg. To some extent, these differences reflect variations in the costs of living in those countries, but the setting of national minimum wages is always a political question too.

Indeed, critics argue that national minimum wages can actually increase poverty if they prevent jobs from being created or lead to employers laying off workers because increased wage costs would render jobs no longer profitable. It is because of such fears that arguments to increase the level of the minimum wage (or to introduce one altogether) often face such opposition. As an alternative, in some countries, such as the UK and US, the minimum wage remains modest, but tax credits are used instead to top up the wages of some low-income households.

Table 3.2: National minimum wages, € per month

Belgium	1,501.8
Netherlands	1,469.4
Ireland	1,461.9
France	1,430.2
United Kingdom	1,249.9
United States	952.5
Slovenia	783.7
Spain	752.9
Greece	683.8
Portugal	565.8
Turkey	415.5
Poland	392.7
Slovakia	337.7
Hungary	335.3
Estonia	320
Czech Republic	318.1
Lithuania	289.6
Latvia	286.7
Bulgaria	158.5
Romania	157.5

Notes: National minimum wage applicable for all employees, or a large majority of employees, in the country. Minimum wages are gross amounts before the deduction of income tax and social security contributions, which vary by country. Data refers to 2013.

Source: Eurostat.

However, in-work benefits suffer from the same problems as the means-tested benefits we discussed in Chapter 2.

Another issue for countries implementing ALMPs is the *sustainability of employment*. Many countries have put mechanisms in place to ensure that job placement is not only short-term, for high return rates of unemployed people to active labour market programmes of different sorts would certainly not be a positive policy outcome. One could also argue that it is not enough to simply place the most vulnerable in society into employment without offering some form of additional mentoring in order to ensure that they can cope with their new life situations. On a similar note, state subsidies to encourage the employment of the long-term unemployed, to protect national companies (or sectors) from international competition or to save businesses from bankruptcy are often popular among the electorate, but opponents of such initiatives have argued that they are not always beneficial in the long run as they can be detrimental to the prospects of other companies in the same industrial branch and so weaken the economy overall. In addition, evaluations of state subsidies for employers have shown that they have not always been very successful in helping the jobless into permanent employment.

Of course, as noted earlier, the state itself is a major employer, and temporary employment programmes in the public sector such as public works schemes can be used to help unemployed citizens sharpen their skills or demonstrate their readiness for work to potential employers. More concretely, the state can also choose to expand employment in the public services. This has the advantage of creating secure, well-paid and skilled jobs. However, the public sector in general has been attacked in recent years and most governments have been under pressure to reduce public sector employment. Indeed, one of the areas of work that some countries have transferred into the private sector has been the delivery of services to help the unemployed back into work (see Box 3.3).

Box 3.3: Public or private? Employment services in the Netherlands

The majority of this chapter has focused on the ways in which the state can use its power to boost both the quantity and the quality of jobs. However, we should not overlook the fact that, ultimately, the private sector makes many of the key decisions that determine the overall levels of employment in society. In practice, the activities of the state interlink with the activities of private businesses in this field of policy and there are some difficult questions about where the boundaries of public – as opposed to private – activities should lie. As we have noted, in its attempts to guard employment, the state can subsidise businesses or even nationalise them, but in so doing, it can have a negative impact on other competing or related businesses.

Recent years have witnessed a rolling back of the state's role in some areas of employment policy, but one particularly interesting – and, perhaps, unusual – development has been the privatisation of employment services themselves in some countries. In the Netherlands, for instance, reforms have seen the services for those who are hardest to place in employment transferred from the state-managed WERKbedrijf offices (formerly the Centre for Work and Income [CWI]) to a series of private organisations. These private companies receive payment from the state partly on the basis of the number of clients referred to them, partly on the basis of the sorts of services they provide and partly on the basis of whether or not the client is successfully placed into employment. The services they offer cover the same kinds of activities provided by state employment agencies, such as training, job-search advice and post-employment mentoring, but one of the aims of the policy is to encourage a diversity of competing providers able to offer a more diverse and flexible range of programmes that reflect that diverse needs of jobseekers. Electronic services for the unemployed have been expanding, while the actual number of WERKbedrijf has recently been considerably reduced (Weishaupt, 2014). Evidence regarding the impact of the reforms has so far been mixed – in part, because contracts have proved too complex and activities difficult to monitor – but the tendering and contracting for the private provision of (public) employment services is now a clear feature of the Dutch system.

This brings us to the last and possibly most important point of the discussion. Some have argued that generous forms of social security, strong labour market regulations and high public spending are no longer sustainable in times of globalisation. In order to remain attractive for foreign investment and to achieve necessary productivity gains in the future – so goes the argument – social security has to become leaner and labour markets more flexible. Across the high-income countries of the OECD, employment policy becoming 'lean' and 'flexible' means many being deprived of social rights that were offered to past generations. There are many arguments advanced by those who see this as part of a necessary modernisation process in order to maintain the levels of wealth and overall employment in these countries. We have addressed what lies behind these arguments in the previous sections of this chapter. We have also shown that employment policy in the broad sense plays a major role in promoting both economic prosperity and social well-being.

Yet, the complexity and interaction of different policy mechanisms makes it very difficult indeed to evaluate and separate the outcomes of single measures; indeed, we are only beginning to really understand many of the long-term effects of certain macroeconomic and social policies. The empirical evidence for many of the crucial policy dilemmas raised in this section is still inconclusive. Answers to whether one or another employment policy is preferable are often 'political', as are answers to whether a 'lean' or a 'generous' welfare state is more conducive to economic growth and the creation of jobs. While globalisation has undoubtedly changed the conditions under which national employment policies have to function today, answers as to how to react to these changes are still disputed. It is likely that trade union and employer association representatives have a very different idea about the policy solutions indeed.

KEY POINTS SUMMARY

■ Employment policy is often reduced to a distinction between passive and active labour market programmes; however, this is a simplification of a much broader field of policy.

■ The main goal of employment policy is to reach and maintain high employment rates under acceptable working conditions.

■ Employment policy can be divided into supply- and demand-side measures, but the emphasis in recent years has been on the former.

■ Long-term unemployment is still among the most significant factors causing poverty; however, job placement alone does not always end this condition.

■ Globalisation has triggered a hard-fought debate about competitiveness and social security; while the empirical evidence is somewhat inconclusive, the preference of the two is still – primarily – a political decision.

KEY READING GUIDE

Sykes (2012) and Deacon and Patrick (2012) cover issues of employment/ unemployment and the intersection of economic and social policy. Hill and Irving (2009: ch 6) and Griggs (2014) offer a slightly different approach to discussing active labour market programmes in the UK and Europe. Comprehensive syntheses of work and welfare policy in the UK and beyond are also provided in Alcock et al (2008: ch 16), Blakemore and Warwick-Booth (2013: ch 7) and Vickerstaff (2012b).

A series of recent publications concentrate on particular employment issues and employment policy user groups. Grover and Piggott's (2015) *Disabled people, work and welfare* critically discusses welfare conditionality and its impact on workless disabled people by means of several country case studies of recent policy changes. Kröger and Yeandle's (2014) *Combining paid work and family care* is interested in the interconnections between work and home life and, again, offers an international perspective by means of comparative Western European and East Asian country case studies. Shildrick et al's (2012) *Poverty and insecurity. Life in low-pay, no-pay Britain* focuses on economic insecurity and demonstrates how the life histories of working-class communities in the UK have been severely affected by labour market changes. Finally, the relationship between employment, health and well-being is discussed in Vickerstaff et al's (2012) *Work, health and wellbeing: the challenges of managing health at work.*

Internet resources on international economic development are relatively easy to find. Readers interested in statistics on GDP growth, inflation rates, unemployment and structural changes in labour markets will find a library of statistical information on the Web: the ILO's labour statistics (LABORSTA), the International Monetary Fund's (IMF's) World Economic Outlook (see: www.imf.org/) and the OECD's Annual Labour Force Statistics and Employment Outlook (see: www.oecd.org) all provide similar statistics. On a smaller scale geographically, the Statistical Bureau of the European Union (EUROSTAT) (see: http://epp.eurostat.ec.europa.eu/) and the Asian Development Bank (see: www.adb.org) also provide very useful statistics on labour markets and labour market transitions. Besides providing numerical information, the ILO has also been concerned with monitoring and bettering the conditions of workers around the world – its webpage (available at: http://ilo.org) contains a list of valuable publications for students interested in the link between employment and social protection. Similarly, the OECD provides timely discussions, research reports and news articles on contemporary employment issues on its webpage (available at: www.oecd.org/employment/).

4

education

Introduction

Access to education is a fundamental human right. Article 26 of the Universal Declaration of Human Rights (United Nations General Assembly, 1948) stresses that every child should have access to free elementary education. In addition, it states that professional education should be made 'generally available' and that access to higher education should be 'determined by merit only' and not subject to racial, gender, religious or any other form of discrimination. Article 26 continues by emphasising that education ought to be 'directed to the full development of the human personality', the 'strengthening of respect for human rights', the 'promotion of understanding, tolerance and friendship' and, eventually, 'the maintenance of peace'.

In reality, education policy is developed with both *social* (even *cultural*) and *economic* goals in mind. Indeed, it has been suggested that the economic significance of education is greater than ever because of a global transition towards 'knowledge-based societies', in which intellectual innovation becomes the primary means to secure economic growth. In recent years, education policy has increasingly been at the centre of debates regarding the competitiveness of national economies, labour market participation, social inclusion and social cohesion. In this sense, education policy is very similar to the pillars discussed in Chapter 1.

Due to this diversity of policy aims – and this is also similar to the previously discussed pillars of social policy – what exactly is meant by 'education policy' can be hard to pin down. Most typically, education policy has been conceptualised by means of a division into three main levels or stages of education: from the fundamental stages in the pre-primary and primary education sector that cater for the youngest children; to secondary education, which provides the main focus of formal schooling, not least in terms of the formal qualifications that school leavers are expected to gain; and, finally, to tertiary education, which caters for those who study beyond the school level by, for instance, undertaking university-level qualifications. The actual ages at which students typically pass from primary to secondary and then to tertiary education can vary considerably across countries and there are major differences between countries in terms of how education services are structured at each of these levels.

The scale and importance of education policies can be crudely indicated by the large amounts of public money that most governments allocate to this field of activity (see Table 4.1). In high-income countries, an average of around 6.5% of gross domestic product (GDP) is devoted to education spending by governments, although the actual figures range from just below 4% in places like Japan to around 7% in some of the Scandinavian countries; upper-middle-income countries display similar patterns, with some – such as Namibia – also devoting very large amounts of national income to education. In the lower- and lower-middle-income countries, however, much more variation in spending is evident, with some – such as Moldova or Kenya – devoting very large amounts of national income to education, while others – such as Georgia and India – allocate rather modest proportions of GDP.

In most countries, the state is the main provider of education. However, a mixed economy of provision is the reality in most places, with public provision being supplemented by private activity. As we will see later in this chapter, the public–private mix in education shows some important variation across the globe, for while many of the highest-spending nations – particularly in Scandinavia – source almost all education spending from public funds, there are other countries – for example, the US, South Korea and Chile – in which substantial private spending plays a hugely significant role alongside public spending.

Table 4.1: Public education expenditure, as % of GDP

High-income countries	
Norway	6.9
Finland	6.8
United States	5.4
Japan	3.9
Upper-middle-income-countries	
Namibia	8.4
Thailand	7.6
South Africa	6.6
Brazil	5.8
Lower-middle-income countries	
Moldova	8.4
Ghana	8.1
India	3.4
Georgia	2.0
Lower-income countries	
Kenya	6.7
Tanzania	6.2
Nepal	4.7
Central African Republic	1.2

Notes: GDP = gross domestic product. Data refers to 2010–12.

Source: World Bank (2014).

While education is usually thought of in terms of the activity that takes places in schools, colleges and universities, a broader definition might also encompass various forms of (on-the-job) vocational training and (non-vocational) 'lifelong' adult learning (see Box 4.1). Future-oriented research and development activities conducted by research centres belonging to private companies or state agencies may have real significance for the education and skills development of nations too. If 'human development' is one of the core goals of education, one may even ask whether public libraries, museums and other cultural institutions (operas, theatre) fall under the realm of education policy.

Box 4.1: Continuing participation in education and training in comparative perspective

In 2003, the European Commission published its final assessment of the Second Continuing Vocational Training Survey (European Commission, 2003). This survey included around 76,000 businesses across the 25 European Union (EU) member countries. It uncovered some striking differences in the provision of, and access to, continuing vocational training schemes across the EU.

Two forms of continuing vocational training were distinguished in the report: first, 'classical' forms of continuing vocational training, which include courses, workshops and seminars offered both within and outside of enterprises; and, second, 'other' forms of continual vocational training, which include instructions by colleagues, as well as job adjustment, rotation and exchange programmes.

Only about half of the businesses surveyed actually offered internal or external training courses to their employees. This average masks stark inequalities. The percentage of employers offering such courses was above 80% in Denmark, Sweden, the Netherlands and Norway compared to only below 25% in most of the new Eastern European accession states, as well as Portugal and Greece, at the time of the survey.

By combining information from the EU's Labour Force Survey and Adult Education Survey (Eurostat, 2014), we know that the participation rate in education and training for 55–64 years olds still varies considerably today. While the merits of lifelong learning programmes have been highlighted by professionals, politicians and academics alike, the reality looks somewhat bleaker, with only about 30% of this age group engaging in some form of formal or non-formal education and training across the EU in 2011. The countries with the highest rates reached participation figures between 40% and 60%, but for the majority of countries, this rate was around or even well below 20%. While the data tells us that many 'did not need' continuing education or training for work or personal reasons, the main obstacles to participation were due to time constraints, that is, conflicts with work or family responsibilities, or the fact that appropriate training was not available close to people's homes, necessary employer support was lacking, it was too costly or it did not match the skills level that people had to begin with.

There is clearly room to improve the availability and access to continuing education and training for many workers and employees and to make the ideal of an ever-improving skills base of the European workforce a reality.

Key policy goals

At the most basic level, education policy is designed to enable citizens to interact with society. In other words, education equips individuals to engage with their 'culture' – that is, the prevalent ideas, norms and beliefs in a given country. Education is not only a tool to 'socialise' children and young people, but also enables individuals to participate in societal or political processes. The historical development of education in European societies can be interpreted against this context. For instance, demands to make education available across all parts of society were closely linked with political struggles for greater democratisation (and vice versa) that took place in many European nations in the 19th century. In many nations, the expansion of democracy was accompanied by an expansion of education, not least because many governments recognised that if all citizens are to participate politically, then they require an education in order to make informed choices. At the same time, by favouring or promoting a particular language or religion, the expansion of education also helped to create a common 'identity' and was at the heart of nation-building processes in 18th- and 19th-century Europe. In short, from the earliest days of state expansion into the field of education, its role in promoting social cohesion has been recognised by policy makers.

Article 26 of the Universal Declaration of Human Rights (United Nations General Assembly, 1948) aligns education policy closely with the issue of human development. From a global perspective, although not uncontested, the so-called United Nations (UN) Human Development Index has become one of the main tools to measure human development. Central to this index is the measurement of educational outcomes (particularly the mean and expected years of school enrolment), for the UN regard access to a decent education as an essential human right on the grounds that it plays a crucial role in allowing humans to develop and fulfil their potential. The average years of education received by people aged 25 and above in high human development countries, that is, the mean years of schooling, is typically between 10 and 12 years. In low human development countries, the respective figures plummet to around 3–5 years. It is not unusual for the number of years of schooling that a child of school entrance age can expect to receive, that is, the expected years of schooling, to be around 7–8 years in some of the lowest-income countries compared to up to 18–19 years in some high-income countries (UNDP, 2014).

Education also has an important economic role. The term 'human capital' is used as shorthand for the skills and qualifications possessed by individuals in the labour market. It has been used since the late 1950s, initially by economists, who argue that – similar to investments in 'material capital', such as factories or machines – employers can achieve additional productivity gains by educating and training their workforce. For governments, increased education spending can be viewed as economic investment if it increases the level of human capital within the labour market. We should note that there is an individual component here too: an individual who enhances their own education and skills can often command higher income in the labour market as a consequence.

Some have argued that education is becoming a more integral part of the economic and social strategy of national governments as a consequence of globalisation. The argument goes that high-income countries, in particular, must have extensive education policies in order to maintain their *competitive economic advantage in global markets* because they cannot compete with some of their low-wage competitors in terms of low manufacturing costs and taxation levels. Consequently, it is suggested, maintaining and enhancing the output of new industrial patents and other intellectual property is crucial to preserving levels of employment and affluence in these countries. To this end, delivering highly specialised, world-leading research via the education system can be an important part of a nation's economic innovation strategy.

However, we should also note that the prolongation of students' time spent in the education system – for instance, by increasing the average minimum time to graduation in secondary and tertiary education or by encouraging more people to attend university – has led to a reduction of labour supply in some countries. Employers' organisations often stress that skills and qualifications gained through education should correspond with those demanded in national economies. Indeed, the fact that, today, some labour markets are characterised by difficulties for employers in filling job vacancies while, at the same time, many people remain unemployed for long spells suggests that they might have a point. From an economic perspective, matching skills with labour market needs might also be an important goal of education policy and many governments try to influence the content of education curricula to this end. In particular, some nations stress the *vocational* dimensions of education much more strongly than others.

Education policy also has some much broader social aims. It is often argued that in a 'fair' society, the economic rewards that individuals reap (ie income) ought to be grounded, in some loose way, in merit. For liberal theorists, this can only be so if there is a broad 'equality of opportunity' in society. By giving all an 'equal start' in life, freely available universal education is seen by some as the guarantor of a broad equality of opportunity. Put bluntly, in an ideal world, it should be educational attainment (or 'merit') that determines a young person's future working career and not simply their family background.

However, such an argument only holds true if there is considerable 'social mobility' in a nation. This term refers to individuals' ability to move across the hierarchical social class system of societies; the term depicts both upwards and downwards movement within individuals' own lifetime or from one generation to another. While the exact definition of 'social class' may vary in the literature, members of 'higher' classes are usually described by higher standards of living and professional qualifications (leading to more secure and more highly paid jobs). While it is generally accepted that education is a major factor in mediating social mobility, as we will see later, many theorists point to broader obstacles to mobility that prevent more education from being a magic wand that can deliver equality of opportunity. Moreover, some even suggest that education itself can be such an obstacle, for if the education system favours the already well-off – for example, because access to the best schools or universities is geared towards those from higher-income backgrounds – then qualifications may reinforce or even exacerbate divisions between social classes rather than ameliorate them. Consequently, some have argued that the 'equality of opportunity' perspective is flawed if there is not some evidence of a broader 'equality of outcome' in terms of which groups of people are gaining educational awards and rewards.

All this points to the multifaceted and, in some cases, potentially conflicting goals of educational policy. Indeed, different nations place differing degrees of emphasis on these different goals. While, compared to social security (see Chapter 2), there is much less consensus among theorists in terms of what different 'types' of education system might look like in high-income countries, we can offer a broadly similar classification. For convenience, we will use the same labels that we used in Chapter 2.

First, there are social democratic types. In these countries, education is largely state-funded and universally available and there is relatively strong social mobility. From the upper-secondary education level onwards, strong vocational education routes typically exist for young people alongside academic education. There is a strong concern with equality of outcome, with high education spending being matched by high social spending more generally. Sweden and Denmark are good examples.

Second, there are liberal types. Here, the state devotes considerable levels of finance to education – albeit usually below levels in the social democratic types – but this is supplemented by considerable private expenditure so that, overall, a very high proportion of GDP is accounted for by education. As, in part, this private expenditure generally favours the better off, but also because lower levels of social spending mean that social inequality tends to be higher, there is less concern with equality of outcome in these nations and social mobility tends to be relatively low. Vocational training routes for young people tend to be underdeveloped. The US is a good example.

Finally, there are corporatist types. Here, the state tends to devote lower levels of national income to education than in the other two types, but relatively high social spending more generally means that inequality is not so high as in liberal types and social mobility is also greater. That said, there is typically a strong division between those undertaking academic and vocational education in these nations, with the latter being tied quite directly to labour market needs. Germany is a good example.

Hidden behind these cross-national differences are important differences in the key delivery mechanisms of education policy. It is to these differences that we now turn.

Key delivery mechanisms

Until recently, 'education' has not featured as prominently as might be expected in the Social Policy literature. While the structure of this textbook has been inspired by Esping-Andersen's (1990) argument that we can find three different 'worlds of welfare', his seminal book did not mention 'education' at all. Similarly, while the Organisation for Economic Co-operation and Development (OECD) has collected a wide range of statistics on different education systems, these are presented separately from its data on social protection, the labour market and healthcare. Statistics on social policy expenditure and financing collected by international organisations such as the OECD and International Labour Organisation (ILO) have, rather bizarrely, not accounted for 'education spending'.

As we noted earlier, in most countries, education consists of a mixed economy of public and private provision. In fact, as Figure 4.1 shows, the breakdown of public and private education funding varies somewhat from place to place. Some of the countries with the highest overall levels of education spending rely almost completely on public sources of funding (eg Finland, Sweden and Belgium). Yet, private education spending is very substantial in many other countries. In the cases of Chile, South Korea and the US, for instance, substantial private spending combines with public spending to bring the overall level of education spending close to or even beyond the spending levels in the aforementioned Scandinavian countries. On average, about 84% of education investment was from the public sector in the industrialised democracies of the OECD. The average for non-OECD countries is generally slightly lower and smaller percentages of funding in these countries come from public bodies. This is indicative of the broader global picture, with private forms of education spending playing, on average, a bigger role in lower-income countries.

An analysis of public and private funding by different levels of education (ie primary, secondary, tertiary) shows a great deal of variation across nations too. Generally, the role of private education is larger in tertiary education than in the other sectors. The cases of Chile, South Korea and the UK are interesting as tertiary education is almost entirely financed by private sources: around 70% of all tertiary education investment comes from private sources in these countries. In countries like Japan and the US, there is still about a 1:2 split of public and private sources of finance for tertiary education spending. By contrast, in other countries – such as Denmark and Finland – close to 95% of tertiary-level spending came from the public sector in the year 2011.

Figure 4.1: Public and private investment in education[a]

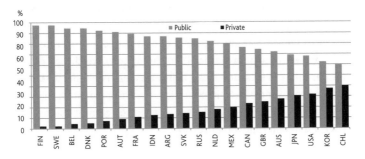

Note: [a] All levels of education, as a percentage of total investment, 2011.

Source: OECD (2014g).

The complex interweaving of public and private funding in most countries is usually matched by a similarly complex interweaving of public and private educational institutions. The most straightforward model comes in the form of state ownership of educational institutions such as schools and universities. In some countries, the state is the dominant provider of education and so most educational institutions are publicly owned. However, such a model is far from the norm. Indeed, privately owned for-profit and not-for-profit schools and colleges are widespread in many countries, and are the dominant forms of provision in some. For instance, churches often run schools that provide a religious education alongside the standard curriculum taught in secular schools. In some countries, ancient seats of learning that pre-date state intervention in education survive as private schools or colleges. While in some countries, such private facilities can only be accessed by those with private funds (ie those with sufficient cash to cover the tuition fees), in others, the state allows the use of public funds to cover some or all of the costs of private education.

Added to this, public educational institutions are, in practice, often given considerable autonomy and act as independent or semi-independent quasi-autonomous non-governmental organisations (QUANGOs). Ancient universities, for instance, often have long-standing legal protections in their statutes that give them some degree of freedom from the state. In other words, the public role can be complex, with the main responsibilities sometimes lying not with the government, but with some other body accountable to it. In the running of schools, for example, head teachers often have a substantial influence on how their school is run, but they also often have to answer to their own school's governing body, which may include some parents and local politicians in its membership. Representatives of other groups interested in education – such as teachers, religious bodies or sometimes even businesses – are often granted the right to participate in different ways too.

For the most part, public education institutions are funded through general taxation. However, recent concerns about the costs of education have led to increased use of co-payments: that is, charges to individual students, usually in the form of tuition fees. This is particularly so for tertiary education, but in many lower-income countries, it is also true for other levels of education. How tuition fees themselves are gathered varies somewhat from place to place. While some countries ask for the upfront payment of fees in cash – which students may have to borrow from family or commercial organisations – many countries either provide the necessary money in the form of a government-funded student loan that is paid back after graduation (often at a favourable rate of interest and only after the student earns a certain level of income) or the money is collected after graduation via a special graduate tax. In some countries, these loans cover living costs as well as tuition fee payments.

Aside from the issues surrounding the financing and formal ownership of educational institutions, education systems can differ considerably in how they organise schooling and a contrast can be drawn between *unitary (comprehensive) systems of schooling*, which emphasise common schooling independent from an individual pupil's attainment, and systems in which *academic selection* underpins the *specialisation and stratification of schooling* rather than a common education.

The Swedish education system provides a good example of a unitary system. Here, all young people are taught in comprehensive schools up to the age of 16 and the unitary character of the school system is broadly retained during the upper-secondary level too. After upper-secondary school, more than a third of Swedish young people continue their studies with universities and higher educational institutions, where a variety of general degrees are available (diploma, bachelor, master). As a complement, upper-secondary vocational education is offered to young people in order to meet the need for more industry-specific skills (Eurydice, 2014). Sweden is similar to other Scandinavian countries (such as Denmark), in which academic selection – and therefore some degree of educational segregation – is institutionalised at a rather late point of individual educational careers.

By contrast, Germany is a prime example of a selective education system. Here, pupils are divided into different types of school as early as age 12. Some unitary schools exist, but pupils normally go on to learn in so-called *Hauptschulen*, *Realschulen* or *Gymnasiums* largely depending on their attainment in primary education. Pupils can receive a first general education qualification at the age of 15 in the *Hauptschule* or a secondary school-level certificate (sometimes called an O-level) at the age of 16 in the *Realschule*. Both of these certificates normally lead to some form of upper-secondary training in vocational schools or on-the-job training in the so-called 'dual system', in which young people spend their time both in vocational schools and also working for their (potential) future employers at the same time. The *Gymnasium* is the typical route for those aspiring to an A-level certificate, which is typically followed by enrolment into higher education with one of the many different (poly)technical, pedagogic and arts colleges or universities. Technical colleges present a route for young people that completed the *Haupt-* or *Realschulen* but decided to continue their education at the tertiary level. In short, rather different educational transitions are put in place for different groups of pupils at a very early stage of their educational careers (Eurydice, 2014).

There are other important variations in how nations organise schooling that it is worth shedding some light on. For instance, we might want to look at the length of education – or overall school-life expectancy – that is typical for each nation. As we can see from Table 4.2, the actual age at which the majority of young people leave the education system varies considerably across countries. Turkey, together with Mexico, appear to be most 'unequal' in our small sample as about 40–50% of 15–19 year olds were no longer enrolled in the education system. Only about 10% of all young people in their 20s had the chance to study at the tertiary level in Mexico too. The vast majority of countries for which such data is available keep their young people in education until they reach the ages of 18 and 19. Among high-income countries, Italy, the UK and the US are an exception as educational participation rates drop to a comparatively low 80% for 15–19 year olds. Conversely, in Denmark and Finland, 40% or more of 20–29 year olds remain in either upper-secondary or tertiary education; these high figures compare to merely around 20% in countries like Italy, France and the UK. Obstacles to higher-level primary school enrolment remain particularly significant in many middle- and low-income countries (see Box 4.2).

Another way of approaching the typical length of education in a country is to examine the working-age population by their *highest level of educational attainment*; this indicator does not emphasise total years in education, but the highest achieved certificate, and the two do not necessarily have to correspond. Table 4.3 shows that the educational attainment of 25–64 year olds continues to vary across high- and upper-middle-income countries. In the most educated nations, 45–50% of the adult population completed tertiary education and around 35–40% completed upper-secondary certificates (eg see Canada, the US and Korea in Table 4.3). Russia is the only non-OECD country that reached similar levels in 2012.

A separate look at tertiary education is interesting as it shows that several OECD countries seem to be lagging behind. Germany and the Czech Republic, among others, had the highest upper-secondary completion rates of the adult population in the OECD in 2012 but tertiary education attainment remained below 30%. Education systems in these countries have come under some criticism for not expanding the numbers of students in higher education in recent years. Some analysts have taken these figures as proof that the according education systems have not adapted adequately to the challenges of globalisation

Table 4.2: Educational participation as a percentage of the population by age group, from age group 3–4 to age group 30–39

	Ages 3–4	Ages 5–14	Ages 15–19	Ages 20–29	Ages 30–39
Denmark	97	99	87	43	9
Finland	55	96	86	42	16
Netherlands	91	100	93	36	5
Australia	47	100	87	35	14
Germany	93	99	90	33	4
Korea	86	99	87	31	2
Norway	96	99	87	30	7
New Zealand	91	100	83	29	11
Argentina	57	100	73	28	9
Chile	62	94	76	28	5
United States	52	97	81	27	6
Hungary	84	98	93	27	4
Czech Republic	70	99	90	26	4
Switzerland	22	99	84	25	4
Turkey	12	95	59	24	4
Brazil	49	95	78	22	8
Italy	94	99	81	21	3
France	99	99	84	21	3
United Kingdom	95	98	78	19	7
Mexico	63	100	53	13	4

Notes: Full-time and part-time students in public and private institutions. Sorted by the educational participation of 20–29 year olds. Data refers to 2012.

Source: OECD (2014g).

and the emerging 'knowledge economy'. There are also other OECD countries in which below upper-secondary education attainment remains stubbornly high: Italy and Portugal show rates in excess of 40%, which means that they are closer to non-OECD countries such as Brazil, but also China and Indonesia, according to this measure.

Table 4.3: Educational attainment of 25–64 year olds

	Below upper-secondary	Upper-secondary	Tertiary
Russian Federation	5.7	40.8	53.3
Canada	10.9	36.5	52.6
United States	10.7	46.3	43.1
Korea	17.6	40.7	41.7
United Kingdom	21.8	37.1	41.0
Finland	15.2	45.1	39.7
Switzerland	13.7	49.7	36.6
Netherlands	26.6	39.0	34.4
France	27.5	41.6	30.9
Germany	13.7	58.2	28.1
Greece	31.5	41.8	26.3
Poland	10.4	65.1	24.5
Czech Republic	7.3	73.2	19.3
Portugal	62.4	18.7	18.5
Mexico	62.7	19.2	18.1
Chile	42.5	39.6	17.8
Italy	42.8	41.5	15.0
Brazil	55.1	31.9	13.0
Indonesia	71.1	21.1	7.9
China	77.7	18.7	3.6

Note: Sorted by tertiary-level attainment. Data refers to 2012.

Source: OECD (2014g).

Box 4.2: Obstacles to higher primary school enrolment in middle- and low-income countries

The development of basic education in lower-income countries has been at the forefront of initiatives for sustainable development and the delivery of essential human rights. While progress has been impressive – helped by large sums of money invested by both national governments and international aid – education quality and equity and gender equality is still lacking in some countries (Unesco and Unicef, 2013). Some of the reasons for this typically identified are as follows:

- In many cases, parents are exposed to a decision about the 'opportunity costs' of schooling – that is, they have to evaluate the costs of sending their child to school and compare this to its expected future income. Direct costs to consider are those for school uniforms, books, tuition fees and so on. The loss of a potential source of income or the loss of the child's support for family or farm work is an important factor too.
- Male and female differentials in literacy and school enrolment remain substantial in many middle- and low-income countries. Cultural and religious attitudes towards women's role in society can play a crucial role here. Education is one of the primary means of gaining access to formal employment. At the same time, access to formal employment is often limited for women, which does not make their education seem worthwhile for many families.
- The relevance of education programmes is not always a given for males as well. Attempts to emulate approaches in high-income countries may come at the cost of disregarding local economic realities and the lack of certain employment opportunities.
- The quality of many schools is still poor. Inadequate support and the poor qualification of teachers are blamed for comparably high rates of repetition of classes and for high numbers of dropouts. The high numbers of repeaters is conducive to the overcrowding of classes – thus spurring a vicious circle and

increasing the risk for parents who consider sending their child to school.

■ According to calculations by the United Nations Educational, Scientific, and Cultural Organization (Unesco), many middle- and low-income countries will continue to depend on international aid to extend basic education programmes. The dependency on external donors may favour short-term policy programmes to increase the reach of basic education over longer-term goals.

A large part of the reluctance to expand higher education may be a result of the very costly nature of highly specialised tertiary education. Indeed, a growing trend within the OECD has been for governments to share the cost of higher education with students themselves, most notably, by charging tuition fees. Significantly, these fees vary substantially across countries: some countries do not have tuition fees for full-time students at all; others do not have them for public, but do for private, institutions; finally, in some countries, students have to pay irrespective of whether they go to a public or private institution. Where they do exist, annual average tuition fees for public institutions range from below US$350 in Turkey and some first degree programmes in France to up to around US$4,000 in Australia and Canada. In Ireland, Japan, South Korea and the US, tuition fees reached between US$5,000 and US$6,500 on average in the academic year 2011 (OECD, 2014g). (We should note that the term average needs to be properly understood here, for the levels of annual tution fees can be well in excess of US$18,000 in the some of the most expensive US universities.)

Naturally, a representation of tertiary education without considering that students may receive benefits from public loans or scholarships/grants in support of tuition fees or living costs is somewhat incomplete. Although no tuition fees were charged in Norway and Sweden, for instance, around 70% of all students still received support in the form of public loans and scholarships/grants. In Australia, we find that just over 80% of the home student body received public loans, while in Chile, Japan and New Zealand, this figure was between 30% and 50%.

At the same time, about 20–40% of students in France, Ireland and the US were supported financially by scholarships/grants; these are figures for public sector institutions – the corresponding rates for private institutions are mostly closer to 80% and 100% (OECD, 2014g).

Key policy issues

An individual's education is among the main determinants of both working careers and unemployment across high-income countries and the importance of educational qualifications has been heightened with the emergence of knowledge economies. Historically, lower-skilled workers have shared in the overall growth in affluence during much of the post-war period by receiving relatively generous wage increases and maintaining relatively secure work contracts. Broader changes in industrial production have resulted in many industrial jobs becoming redundant (see also Chapter 3) and so the percentage of the labour force employed in the agricultural and industrial sectors has decreased from just above 50% in 1960 to just above 25% in 2011 in the OECD countries. As a consequence, individuals with low skills, who in the past would have found a stable 'haven' in these sectors, often have to be content with low-paid, often precarious jobs in the service industry. This is certainly a somewhat simplified version of nearly 60 years of progressions in political economies. However, some figures may help to underline the significance of these changes.

For instance, the percentage of low-qualified people without completed vocational training among the unemployed has been comparatively high in the Czech Republic and other Eastern European countries. The unemployment rates for university and technical college graduates in these countries have been below 4% throughout the last decade. At the same time, the proportion of unemployed people without completed vocational training has remained above 20%. In other words, the risk of employees without high levels of education or advanced vocational training being permanently excluded from the labour market is comparatively high. This pattern of unemployment risk is by no means unique in the Czech Republic and other Eastern

European countries. In 2012, the average unemployment rate for individuals with lower-secondary education was close to 15% across the OECD, while the rate for those with a tertiary degree was merely 5%. Such gaps appeared to be particularly pronounced in nations with educational systems that institute a strong and early division between the academic and vocational education of young people, but so-called 'skill-biased technological change' – a shift in rewards of employment that favours those with very specialised skills in the new knowledge-based economy – has been identified by economists as a major factor in explaining rising income inequality in OECD nations.

Indeed, Figure 4.2 illustrates that educational attainment has a substantial impact on individual earnings. In all of the countries in the chart, we can see that those whose formal education finished at below upper-secondary school level are much more likely to have low earnings (defined as at or below half of the national median income) than those who complete tertiary education. This point has been made in the economics literature for some time now. Cross-national research in this field has uncovered striking relationships between educational attainment and the wage levels of the working population, with those looking back at relatively short careers in education finding themselves increasingly more likely to be in the growing low-paid sector of the labour market.

We should not, however, presume that more education is necessarily an effective route to tackling poverty and inequality. Indeed, while some hail education as the most important component of social policy in the 21st century, there is much to suggest that education can actually play a role in increasing social divisions. This is likely to be particularly so if educational opportunities are not equally available to all or if the benefits of education are more likely to be accrued by the already better off, and for the most part, this seems to be so. Indeed, a recent cross-national analysis of educational attainment in OECD countries (the Programme for International Student Assessment [PISA]) found that, in some countries, there were significant variations in the performance of pupils (see Figure 4.3). Different individual family backgrounds, as

Figure 4.2: Low earnings[a] and educational attainment

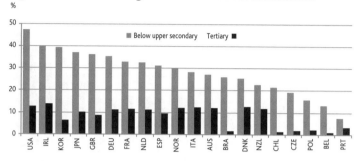

Note: [a] Percentage of adults with below upper secondary or tertiary education living at or below half of median income, 2012

Source: OECD (2014g).

well as the school environment of these pupils, could account of much of this variation.

Put more simply, in many countries, there seems to be a clear social stratification of schooling, with better-off pupils attending better-achieving schools, suggesting that equality of opportunity is far from a reality in most countries. Importantly, the countries in which this kind of stratification was minimised were primarily those in which a unitary (or comprehensive) model of education existed. Similar evidence is emerging with respect to social mobility, recent data showing that the Scandinavian nations have much higher levels of social mobility than the US and UK in particular. In the UK, moreover, there is strong evidence to suggest that social mobility has actually declined in recent years partially because of the strong link between parental income and a child's educational attainment (see Box 4.3).

From a macroeconomic perspective, numerous international organisations have emphasised the relationship between educational attainment and economic growth. Some scholars have shown that the average years of primary and secondary schooling across high- and low-income countries

Figure 4.3: Student performance[a] in mathematics

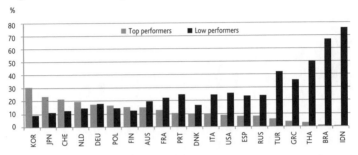

Note: [a] Percentage of students at or above proficiency level 5 (Top performers) and below proficiency level 2 (Low performers), 2012.

Source: OECD (2014f).

are positively correlated with annual growth rates of GDP – that is, those countries in which a higher share of the working population completed primary and secondary school certificates have consistently done better in terms of their economic performance compared to those with comparatively lower levels. Similar patterns have been uncovered for the relationship between economic growth and education spending. The argument that education delivers growth is thereby based on the fundamental assumption that economically advanced, productive nations are in need of a lot of educated individuals. Also, technological progress is said to rely on innovations from top-class universities and research laboratories. Korea and Singapore are commonly presented as prime examples of countries in which governments have intervened massively in education policy and in which economic growth rates have surpassed those of many of their competitors since the early 1980s.

However, the relationship between school enrolment and economic growth is not deterministic and we should be wary of presenting education as a 'magic bullet' for economic policy. If we only concentrate on the high-income countries of the OECD, for instance, the clear link between educational attainment and economic performance found in some research becomes less straightforward: in fact, the evidence shows that numerous OECD countries deviate from this pattern of high education spending producing high economic growth. Among middle- and low-income countries, similar problematic cases can be found and scholars have underlined that not all 'Asian tigers' have invested heavily in education in the way Korea or Singapore did and yet they still achieved similar economic growth rates (eg Hong Kong and China). Other developing countries around the world have made similar attempts to expand the overall educational attainment of their labour force without gaining significant economic progress (eg Egypt and Sri Lanka).

Box 4.3: Education and social mobility in the UK

We should be wary of presuming that education always acts as a tool for enhancing social mobility or promoting equality of opportunity. Indeed, recent evidence from the UK has pointed to the significant role that rising educational attainment has played in impacting and, at times, even *reducing* the level of social mobility.

Comparing people born in 1958 with those born in 1970, researchers found that for the latter group, earnings at age 30 were more closely tied with their parents' earnings during childhood than was the case for those born in 1958 (Blanden et al, 2005). In other words, their position in the income 'hierarchy' was more heavily influenced by their parents' position within it than had been the case for an earlier generation.

In a more recent study comparing people born between 1958 and 1978 with those born after 1991, the researchers also found that educational attainment – measured in terms of the percentage of children reaching Key Stage 2 in English and maths – improved at a faster rate for those from low-income households born after 1986 compared to those from high-income households. This development led to a noticeable reduction of the educational attainment gap at age 16 (Blanden and Macmillan, 2014).

However, when considering *higher*-quality attainment – such as higher education participation or attaining A*–B in three or more A-level subjects – the researchers continue to find no comparable decline in educational inequality between those from low- and high-income households: the share of the most deprived participating in higher education remained firmly at below 3% compared to 22% for the least deprived; considering the attainment of A*–B in three or more A-level subjects, the share of the most deprived remained firmly at around 7% compared to 20–22% for those from high-income households.

While education attainment has been improving across the board, these findings suggest that equality of opportunity is far from a reality in the UK. Supporting young people from low-income households to reach high levels of proficiency at school level – particularly in maths and English – remains a crucial education policy objective. Extending targeted financial support may be an important component of national strategies to engage pupils from low-income family backgrounds. At the same time, investing into programmes that help those young people that struggle to meet national targets at school level promises to improve earnings inequality and social mobility in the UK more broadly.

Even if we put economic considerations to one side and focus purely on academic concerns, the relationship between investment in education systems and educational and economic outcomes is also far from straightforward. The PISA study mentioned earlier found that, for instance, neither public nor private school spending is directly correlated with pupils' proficiency levels in mathematics. In part, this may be because, as a labour-intensive service, much of the spending goes directly on teachers' salaries; the overall level of spending tells us little about the quality of education in terms of class sizes or the standard of equipment within schools, for instance. For governments increasing investment in education, therefore, there are tricky questions to be tackled about how to best guarantee a return on this investment.

Yet, despite the lack of clear evidence about the impact of educational expansion, most countries have looked to extend educational opportunities in recent years. Plans to increase the number of school leavers continuing their education at the tertiary level, along with innovative programmes of lifelong learning and access programmes for mature students, as well as increased numbers of student migrants, have increased university student numbers in many countries. Simultaneously, the importance of early childhood education has gained increased attention in many places, with some countries adopting more generous child benefit programmes and expanding the availability of day nurseries and pre-schools. All this necessitates further investments in the education system. Indeed, the majority of governments around the globe currently share the commitment to increase education spending in order to train and hire more skilled teachers, as well as to build, improve and modernise existing schools and universities.

All this, of course, raises questions about how to finance this expansion, and the introduction of – or the increase in the level of – co-payments in education has been a commonly used solution. Most notably, many OECD countries have introduced or increased the level of tuition fee payments in higher education, but some commentators have expressed worries about the fact that many students have been forced to accumulate considerable amounts of debt at the start of their young working careers. Proponents of tuition fees argue that the additional funds are necessary to attract leading teachers and researchers in highly specialised fields and to improve student–teacher ratios, as well as the quality of and access to libraries and other student resources. By pointing to countries such as the US, Canada and Korea, in which relatively high tuition fees have been paired with high and rapidly increasing tertiary education participation rates, proponents of fee-charging argue that co-payments can be compatible with expanding access to higher education. Yet, there is also some evidence which suggests that when tuition fees are not accompanied by wide-ranging and generous scholarship programmes, those from lower-income backgrounds are often discouraged from studying at the tertiary level, decreasing social diversity in universities (and threatening social mobility) even further. Moreover, there is evidence that the level of fees may be crucial.

At the heart of these debates – and this is where we go full circle and return to the beginning of this chapter – is a major question about the fundamental goals of the education system. Countries with relatively high percentages of private spending in tertiary education typically feature a higher dispersion of teaching quality and student attainment. From a human capital perspective, this may be very desirable. For instance, it can be argued that having a small number of very well-funded elite universities not only produces elite students (sometimes referred to as high achievers), but also has an important role to play in national strategies for producing specialised, cutting-edge research and development that, in turn, leads to the new patents, products, ideas and technologies that bring success in the competitive global knowledge economy. To this end, some countries have, in fact, encouraged a stratification of the university sector by allowing universities to charge variable fees on the basis of a presumed variation in the quality of the institutions themselves. Partly, this is a response to the very high costs of maintaining a world-leading research university, but it is also a strategy that is based on the presumption that some students are more able than others. Reconciling an equitable model education with one that develops the talents of elite scholars is a far from easy task.

KEY POINTS SUMMARY

Education:

- ◼ can play a key role in promoting social cohesion and social mobility;
- ◼ can be selective or unitary;
- ◼ has different functions at the primary, secondary and tertiary levels;
- ◼ is deemed to be an increasingly important economic tool;
- ◼ plays a central role in shaping a nation's human capital;
- ◼ can help boost individuals' financial rewards; and
- ◼ can contribute to inequality and decreasing social mobility.

KEY READING GUIDE

West (2012) and Callender (2012) discuss education in schools and lifelong training and learning programmes, respectively, while Hill and Irving (2009: ch 9) focus their discussion on early child development and tertiary education programmes. Vickerstaff (2012a), Alcock et al (2008: ch 15) and Bochel and Daly (2014: ch 11) provide more general introductions to education policy at various levels of delivery.

Basit and Tomlinson's (2014) *Social inclusion and higher education* provides different perspectives on widening participation programmes in tertiary education, while Sutherland's (2013) *Education and social justice in a digital age* takes a closer look at the impact of educational inequality in times of rapid technological change. Current debates in the field of education policy are also comprehensively discussed in Ball's (2013) *The education debate*. Discussions of recent reforms of the education system in the UK are provided in Mortimore (2014); this book updates the detailed historical account of how the significance of education policy has changed since the 1950s provided in Tomlinson (2005). Castles's (2007) wider discussion in *The disappearing state? Retrenchment realities in an age of globalization* on the functions of states in the 21st century as they try to defend themselves against the global and economic pressures of retrenchment remains relevant and also contains several references to the changing role of education as an economic and social development strategy.

The statistics used in this chapter were taken from several sources that are all available to interested readers on the Internet. Human Development Statistics published by the United Nations Development Project (UNDP) contain data on public and private investment in education for virtually all nations around the globe (see: www.undp.org/). Unesco also publishes a much wider range of information on international education systems in its World Education Indicators database (available at: www.uis.unesco.org/Pages/default.aspx) – statistics on finance, investment, enrolment and, to some extent, attainment can all be found here. The most detailed data on the functioning of education systems are still published in the OECD Education at a Glance reports. The statistics used to inform these period reports – including the latest findings of the PISA studies (OECD, 2014f) – are obtainable from the official OECD webpage (available at: www.oecd.org). Finally, the EU's Encyclopaedia on National Education Systems (Eurypedia) contains excellent country profiles for all its members (see: http://eacea.ec.europa.eu/education/eurydice/eurypedia_en.php).

5

health

Introduction

Healthcare is unquestionably one of the major fields of public and social policy and it is often at the heart of political debate. There are obvious reasons for this, not least the fact that access to healthcare services is vital for our general well-being. Indeed, it is central to our basic human rights – including the right to life – and Article 25 of the Universal Declaration of Human Rights (United Nations General Assembly, 1948) states that both access to medical care and, more generally, a standard of living adequate for health and well-being are fundamental rights.

Despite such acceptance of the importance of healthcare services, in most countries, there is a vigorous debate about the shortcomings and shortfalls of healthcare provision. In part, this is a consequence of the huge potential of modern medicine: continual scientific advances lead to new diagnoses, treatments and interventions and the financial costs of providing all citizens with unlimited and unrestricted access to the full range of healthcare interventions is beyond even the richest of countries (see Box 5.1). In other words, rationing is a feature of healthcare systems. However, it should also be noted that the organisation of healthcare systems fundamentally shapes who has access to the services that are provided. Indeed, inequalities of access are a feature of most healthcare systems and such inequities often form the focal point of debate.

Box 5.1: Ever-expanding demand?

In the early days of state expansion into healthcare, it was believed by some that as access to health services expanded, the level of ill-health in society would drop and, therefore, so would the demand for (and the cost of) healthcare provision. This view proved to be deeply flawed and despite recent concerns with cost containment, healthcare expenditures have expanded in countries with well-developed health systems. There are many reasons for this, but two in particular are worthy of note: *technological advancement* and *population ageing*.

The sheer scale of modern medicine brings more rapid advances in knowledge than was the case in the past. New treatments and procedures are developed with regularity and, indeed, our ability to diagnose medical conditions expands too. While not all advances will increase spending – many, in fact, save money by improving on existing treatments – there is a consensus that, overall, they have contributed heavily to increasing healthcare costs, and it is certainly difficult for government to deny citizens access to new treatments as they become available.

A large part of the costs of technological advancement are indirect: by contributing to our ability to extend life expectancy, medical advances have been one of the causes of the ageing of populations in high-income countries. However, a concern for policy makers is that the average healthcare costs of those aged 65 and over are higher than those for the rest of the population, with some estimates suggesting that they are three to four times greater.

Of course, advances in medical technology and increased life expectancies are very important health policy success stories, so we should avoid dubbing these issues as 'problems', as some people tend to do. Indeed, both may bring greater costs to healthcare systems, but most would agree that these costs are more than balanced by the enormous benefits they bring.

Healthcare policy is typically thought of in terms of medical services delivered by doctors and nurses in hospitals or community health facilities, such as clinics or doctors' surgeries. Such activities are at the heart of healthcare policy, and will form the core of this chapter, but a broader definition would also encompass the services provided by dentists, opticians and pharmacists, and arguably those of medical research scientists too. It might also include the delivery of measures that aim to tackle particular health-related problems (such as obesity or alcohol abuse) through health promotion programmes or that involve planning for potential health hazards and pandemics (such as the outbreak of bird flu). It could encompass attempts to tackle healthcare inequalities such as varying life expectancy rates across a nation through programmes that involve addressing a wide range of underlying issues that affect our physical and mental well-being, such as housing conditions, the quality of the local environment and the distribution of income in society.

The scale and importance of healthcare policies can be illustrated by pointing to their cost (see Figure 5.1). In high-income countries, spending by the government in this area accounted for around 7.5% of gross domestic product (GDP) in 2012. Even in less wealthy countries, government expenditure between 4% and 7% of GDP is not uncommon, although there are many places where expenditure is only around 1% or 2% of GDP. Added to this mix, however, are often very substantial levels of private spending on healthcare. Indeed, in some countries – such as the US – private spending exceeds public spending. When both public and private spending is accounted for, high-income countries allocate, on average, in excess of 12% of their GDP to healthcare, while middle- and low-income countries spend just short of 6% in total. Healthcare is big business around the world.

Key policy goals

At the most basic level, the goal of healthcare policy can be defined as ensuring that citizens have access to adequate medical provision. More often than not, this will be during times of ill-health but medical services are often required as a matter of routine by those who are perfectly healthy (eg during childbirth or vaccination). However, what is deemed adequate medical provision – and how states grant access – varies considerably between nations. Indeed, these variations are often quite stark.

In many countries, the state is the main provider of healthcare services, and in most high-income countries, the state has played a very large role for much of the past 100 years. The expansion of state involvement in healthcare has complex roots, but it was typically in response to the high cost of healthcare provided by the free market, and the subsequent threat to well-being that arose from a widespread lack of access to medical services, that the state expanded its role in the provision of health services. Indeed, economists often point to healthcare as a classic example of market failure as many of those who are in greatest need of medical assistance are those who are least likely to be able to afford it, not least because disease and ill-health hamper an individual's ability to earn money through employment (Glennerster, 2003). However, the expansion of state involvement has taken many different forms. We will examine the detail of the different mechanisms in the next section of this chapter, but, generally speaking, three 'ideal types' can be seen in high-income countries, each with slightly differing goals (Blank and Burau, 2013).

First, there are those nations where the state plays the dominant role in healthcare by acting as a near-monopoly supplier of health services. In these cases, the state owns the majority of healthcare facilities such as hospitals and clinics, employs the majority of medical professionals, and funds services directly through taxes. Typically, because the service is funded through taxation, all citizens are entitled to use the service on the basis of need, not the ability to pay: in other words, there is universal service provision. Such systems view the provision of healthcare as a government or public responsibility and the high levels of public provision crowd out private services, although a modestly sized private sector typically coexists alongside the state system. The universal principles underpinning these systems offer a service that delivers relatively equal access to healthcare and they can be viewed as broadly egalitarian in intent. Systems of this sort exist in the UK and in Sweden and can be broadly dubbed as 'social democratic' systems.

At the other extreme are countries where healthcare is primarily seen as a private responsibility and therefore a matter for the free market. In such cases, individuals in need of treatment will typically receive it in privately owned hospitals and clinics and will be charged for the cost of doing so; patients can cover these costs either by using their own private medical insurance – sometimes provided as part of an employment package – or by paying one-off fees from their own pocket. Consequently, access is determined on the basis of ability to pay: if a citizen cannot afford to pay the fee or does not have insurance to cover the costs, then they will not receive treatment. However, in these cases, the private market is typically supported by a state-organised healthcare safety net. This can take many forms, but often involves the provision of state-organised emergency services to cover unplanned treatments (eg those resulting from accidents) and a state-organised insurance scheme that provides funds for those on low incomes who cannot cover the costs of care themselves or whose insurance scheme will not meet the full costs of treatment. In such instances, public support is usually provided on a means-tested basis: it is available only to those deemed unable to afford the full cost of private cover. The underpinning values of these systems are almost the polar opposite of the social democratic system described earlier. The state aims to stimulate private provision rather than to crowd it out; indeed, the state's role is limited to that of provider of last resort in order to facilitate this and, moreover, equity is not a core concern for the system because major inequities in access necessarily arise when the free market determines what is provided. These systems can be broadly dubbed as 'liberal' systems and the US is a good example of such an approach.

A third option is almost a middle way between the two systems described earlier and involves the state organising a comprehensive social health insurance fund that collects a fixed percentage of all citizens' income via the taxation system. These social insurance schemes are designed to cover the costs of medical treatments incurred by citizens, but the provision of services themselves is often left to the private, voluntary and quasi-governmental sectors, making the system much more sympathetic towards the development of a private health services market than the social democratic model. This differs from the private insurance approach in so far as it allows for a collective pooling of funds so that all citizens can be covered and all pay an equal share of their income. Moreover, because payments are collected through the taxation system, membership of a scheme is compulsory rather than a matter of individual choice. The social insurance–private insurance distinction may seem a fine-grained one, but it is hugely important in practice because the two systems have rather different goals. Unlike private insurance schemes, social insurance-based schemes emphasise the need for the universal coverage of healthcare services and so have some degree of equity built within them. Indeed, they insure against collective risks rather than individual risks. However, unlike the social democratic schemes, greater variation in the nature of services is sometimes permitted because the state's role is limited to the collection of finance. Indeed, some countries allow citizens a choice between different competing social insurance funds, each with different terms of service. As with the social democratic system, there is usually a modestly sized private insurance sector that allows those with higher incomes to join schemes that offer additional levels of protection. This system might be broadly dubbed a 'corporatist' system, and Germany and France have systems like this.

This three-way division has strong parallels to that found in the social security sector (see Chapter 2), and just as Esping-Andersen (1990) argued that there were three worlds of welfare in the field of social security, some have suggested that there are three worlds of healthcare too (Bambra, 2005); therefore, we have used the same labels for the three systems here. In practice, as we noted earlier, public and private sector services coexist in most nations; in other words, most nations offer a mixed economy of provision. However, the state's role varies greatly from that of main provider of healthcare to that of merely funder of a last-resort safety net, a fact reflected in the differing spending patterns shown in Figure 5.1.

Figure 5.1: Public and private expenditure on health[a]

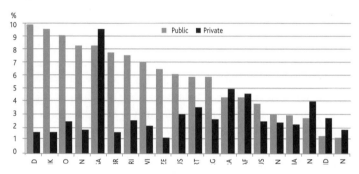

Note: Total health expenditure as a percentage of gross domestic product (GDP), 2012.

Source: World Bank (2014).

Key delivery mechanisms

In examining the key delivery mechanisms in the healthcare sector, it makes sense to break the discussion into two distinct parts: one dealing with *service funding* mechanisms and the other dealing with *service provision* mechanisms. As indicated in the previous section, the state influences both these dimensions of healthcare, although different countries can adopt quite different roles in each. We will begin our discussion by looking at funding mechanisms before going on to look at service provision.

The most basic of service funding mechanisms is for governments to simply use general taxation to fund healthcare policies. In such instances, the government does not establish any special funds to cover the costs of health services or ask citizens to make any specially differentiated tax or social insurance payments towards health services; instead, the government merely treats healthcare as one of many different policy areas competing for a share of its regular tax revenues. Such an approach gives the government a great degree of flexibility over the allocation of funds, allowing it to increase or decrease the amount of monies allocated to the health budget without having to make special adjustments to dedicated healthcare taxes. It also allows the government to easily move funds between different areas of policy if priorities change without, for instance, explaining why it wants to remove surplus funds from a dedicated national healthcare account. This, of course, is not necessarily a strength of the approach: it certainly has the potential to politicise health spending and can make it easy for a hostile government to restrict the funding of health services. On the other hand, it also makes it easy for a sympathetic government to expand funding. For the most part, this is how the UK's National Health Service (NHS) is funded.

However, in many nations, there are tighter restrictions on the state's control over healthcare funds. Indeed, in much of Western Europe, services are funded by dedicated social health insurance funds. In such cases, a proportion of a citizen's earnings must be paid into health insurance funds (eg in Germany, a general rate of 8.2% of earnings has been paid since January 2009), with the state and the citizen's employer usually making a significant contribution too (a common rate of 7.3% of earnings is currently paid by German employers). Although, in effect, a form of taxation – contributions have to be made by law and the government usually sets the contribution levels as part of its regular budgeting process – the allocation of these funds is not usually at the discretion of the government because the contributions have been earmarked for healthcare expenditure. Indeed, in some countries, the funds are managed by non-governmental agencies. While the loss of flexibility in such systems is sometimes bemoaned, there are advantages to such an approach, not least the fact that citizens can see where a substantial part of their tax payments are being directed; indeed, for a government looking to increase welfare expenditure, a proposed rise in social health insurance contributions is usually much less likely to cause a political stir than a rise in the general rate of taxation because people can see a clear link between their increased contribution and actual service provision.

These first two mechanisms are collective or social mechanisms, that is, they involve raising compulsory payments from the public using the government's tax-raising powers. On top of these public forms of funding, most countries also rely on the considerable private financing of health services. First, private health insurance has a wide base in many countries. For-profit and not-for-profit schemes operate in almost every country in the world. As noted earlier, these schemes vary in terms of their market penetration. For instance, in 2012, private health insurance schemes provided 59% of healthcare finance in the US, but in Denmark, they were the source of only 12% of healthcare spending (WHO, 2014). Private health insurance schemes are, in principle, similar to insurance products of any other sort: individual customers pay regular premiums to an insurer in return for coverage against major healthcare risks. As with all insurance products, premiums vary according to the individual customer's exposure to risk, and the level of coverage offered by competing insurers can vary quite widely. Indeed, both the main advantage and disadvantage of private insurance is the more personalised service it offers: relatively healthy people deemed 'good risks' by the insurers may be offered favourable terms of service, including lower premiums, but, conversely, those with a poor health record or long-term illness may find their premiums significantly more expensive on average. In many countries, private insurance schemes act primarily as a supplement to widespread publicly funded healthcare services and, in such cases, the main incentive for individuals to join a private health insurance scheme is usually that it offers a marginal service enhancement, such as more choice over when treatment is offered or greater speed of access to services.

In addition to private insurance schemes, one-off charges or user payments are another important private finance mechanism, be they for surgical procedures, prescription medicines or consultations with medical professionals. These charges can be for access to public services as well as for private ones: although abolished in early 2013, Germany, for instance, saw the requirement of a €10 payment for the first visit to a general practitioner in each quarter, a cost that could not be recouped from social health insurance funds. More common still are charges for non-medical costs that may nonetheless inevitably be incurred during the course of treatment: meals eaten during a stay in hospital for instance.

We should also make it clear that there is often a real blurring of the boundaries between public and private funding in practice. As noted earlier, in many countries, citizens are covered by a patchwork of public and private schemes. Most notably, while contributions to private health insurance funds may appear to be a candidate for a purely private funding source, in practice, many countries offer tax breaks or tax subsidies for private health insurance contributions; as these tax breaks involve the loss of potential tax revenue, they are, in effect, forms of negative government spending. While this may seem a somewhat obscure argument, it should be borne in mind that such subsidies are active government policies, usually introduced to stimulate the take-up of private health insurance.

The complex interweaving of public and private service funding mechanisms in most countries is usually matched by a similarly complex interweaving of public and private service delivery mechanisms. Once again, perhaps the most straightforward mechanism – conceptually at least – comes in the form of state ownership of medical facilities, such as hospitals and clinics. In some countries, the state is the main supplier of medical services of this sort, being responsible for the building, staffing and management of key healthcare institutions.

While state ownership stills forms the backbone of the health service in many countries, even those with a large state sector tend to possess a more complex pattern of public provision in practice. For instance, public hospitals are often placed under the ownership of independent or semi-independent quasi-autonomous non-governmental organisations

(QUANGOs) or, indeed, are QUANGOs in their own right. In the UK, for instance, some public hospitals have been allowed to become 'foundation hospitals', giving them greater autonomy in planning budgets and staffing, including the power to borrow money independently of the government. Added to this, even when the state does staff and manage health facilities, it may often finance the building or purchasing of such facilities through money borrowed from private sources. Indeed, in some countries, it is not uncommon for the state to lease large buildings from private companies. Similarly, private corporations usually provide much of the equipment and medical supplies on which health services rely. Indeed, it is worth noting that the pharmaceuticals market, for instance, is increasingly dominated by a small number of very powerful multinational corporations on whom states depend for the supply of key medications. The power of these corporations can be a particularly acute problem for governments in low-income countries (see Box 5.2).

Box 5.2: The challenges of delivering equitable healthcare in South Africa

The structure of the South African healthcare system has complex roots that emanate from its recent history and, in particular, its transition from a racist Apartheid regime to a modern democracy. During much of the Apartheid era, healthcare policy was itself racist, with separate medical facilities existing for white and black people and funding allocations often unfairly distributed, but in the run-up to the democratic transition in 1994, policy changed and medical services were desegregated. In the period since, significant healthcare reforms have been introduced in order to improve the funding of public services and to expand access to healthcare facilities, with the underlying goal of making healthcare more equitable.

However, the reforms have been far from successful in equalising access and, in practice, significant inequities are widening. As the higher-quality hospitals were already located in white neighbourhoods, an informal geographic barrier to access persists, with many of the best facilities inaccessible or less accessible to many black people. Moreover, public hospitals and clinics are of good quality but are overstretched, and waiting times can be long. Perhaps in part because of this, there has been a considerable expansion of the private healthcare sector in South Africa since the early 1990s, with much of the white population using their greater wealth to purchase private medical insurance and so guaranteeing their access to higher-quality services. Not only has this ensured that an income barrier has replaced a 'race' barrier in recent years, but it has also presented a considerable challenge to the government in terms of human resource management. Lured by the better pay on offer in the private sector, much of the specialist medical labour is deployed in the private sector despite the fact that it caters for a minority of the population. Per capita expenditure on health stands at around US$1,400 in the private and US$140 in the public sector; 40 million, or 84%, of the South African population remain uninsured, while 70% of doctors work in the private sector (Mayosi and Benatar, 2014).

Added to this, the global nature of the medical sector has presented some tricky problems for the South African government. In particular, it has been hit hard by a 'brain drain', with thousands of doctors migrating to high-income countries. In part, this has also been a consequence of efforts to expand access to healthcare. Much of the policy emphasis has been on creating clinics to deliver basic care in previously underserved communities. While this strategy is an essential part of improving healthcare outcomes, the routine nature of much of the work performed in these clinics often does not appeal to highly skilled clinicians keen to develop careers based on medical specialisms. Not only have there been problems in staffing these clinics, but the emphasis on expanding basic care at the expense of specialist care has also been cited by some as a contributory factor in the rising number of doctors migrating.

The global market has also played a significant role in holding back the South African government's plans for improving access to key treatments. The country continues to face real healthcare challenges. Following much international lobbying, deals allowing the manufacture of cheap unbranded generic antiretroviral drugs (ARVs) to be produced locally were agreed in 2002, reducing prices to around US$100 per treatment per year (from previously as high as US$10,000 per person per year at the start of the millennium). In 2004, the South African government instituted a programme for distributing ARVs, and mortality caused by HIV/AIDS (and tuberculosis) dropped from 14 to six per 1,000 persons per year in 2009 (Mayosi and Benatar, 2014).

While access to ARVs has been significantly extended, it is still far from universal and HIV/AIDS stubbornly remains the most burdening disease in South Africa, with 11,201 total years of life (in thousands) being lost in 2012, much higher than the rates for diarrheal diseases (1,139), violence (1,018), tuberculosis (760) and stroke (543) (Institute of Health Metrics and Evaluation, 2014).

In most countries, the private sector plays at least some role in terms of the direct delivery of front-line health services. Again, this role can take many different forms and varies widely in terms of scope. Privately owned for-profit and not-for-profit hospitals and health centres are widespread in most countries, and are the dominant form of provision in some. While, in some countries, such private facilities can only be accessed by those with private funds (ie those with private health insurance or sufficient cash to cover one-off payments), in others, the state allows citizens to receive publicly funded treatments in private healthcare facilities.

Added to this issue of the ownership of key healthcare facilities are often complicated issues about the contractual status of key healthcare professionals, particularly doctors (see Box 5.3). While, in some countries, the majority of doctors are private practitioners, in others, the reverse is true, and in many others, doctors often share their time between public and (the often more lucrative) private practice. While this may seem something of fine-grained issue, it can prove hugely important in policy terms, not least because the degree to which clinicians are under the employ of the state can have a major bearing on the degree to which the state can influence the activity of clinicians. If doctors' main source of income is government-financed, then the political leverage of the state is usually increased.

Whether healthcare organisations are publicly or privately owned, the state always plays an important regulatory role. For example, the state is usually responsible for determining: which drugs are deemed safe to go to market; which treatments (and at what cost) it will fund from public sources; who can legally practice as a doctor and what qualifications they need; and, in more general terms, the legal basis on which competition between private suppliers can take place. The state might also lay down guidelines regarding what standard of treatment individual patients can expect to receive, which treatments are deemed the most effective and, indeed, which suppliers it deems the most trustworthy or of the highest quality. It is in large part through these regulatory activities that the state aims to influence the quality of healthcare provision.

While we have focused the main part of our discussion here on clinical services, we should keep in mind the point we made right at the start of this chapter: that health policy stretches far beyond these boundaries. In particular, public health measures that are designed to prevent the spread of specific illnesses or diseases are vital, be they, for example, vaccination programmes, the banning of harmful drugs, policies for cutting the levels of damaging pollutants or, more generally still, workplace-based health and safety procedures. Added to this, the state can also play an important role in encouraging people to lead more healthy lives. Health promotion programmes aimed at, for instance, persuading people to smoke less, to eat more fruit and vegetables, to practise safe sex, or to exercise regularly have an important role to play in boosting the health of nations. However, public health and health promotion activities usually draw more modest financial support from governments than medically based treatments: in high-income countries, they typically account for little more than around 3% of total healthcare expenditure (OECD, 2014h).

Box 5.3: Paying doctors

Like education (see Chapter 4), a major feature of healthcare services is that they are *labour-intensive*. Much of the healthcare budget consists of payments towards the salary costs of medical professionals, and in most countries, the healthcare workforce forms one of the largest occupational groups in every community. Yet, while all countries require the services of doctors in order to meet the healthcare needs of their citizens, how they procure these services varies significantly. This is particularly true with regard to primary care doctors (often referred to as general practitioners or family doctors), who often work alone or in small groups in small-scale local practices or clinics.

Perhaps the most straightforward mechanism is for general practitioners to be employed directly by the state as *salaried public sector employees*. In such cases, national pay rates are usually negotiated by professional associations, with some variations at the margins allowed to account for increased levels of expertise, specialisation or workload. While such an approach gives the government much certainty in terms of planning its annual labour costs and is easy to organise in administrative terms, fixed national salary levels can sometimes make it difficult to attract general practitioners to work in areas with higher living costs or more challenging workloads. Similarly, fixed national salaries may create disincentives for doctors to take on additional work or to adopt innovative techniques if they are not rewarded for doing so.

At the other extreme are schemes that pay doctors on a *fee-for-service* basis. Here, the government agrees rates it is willing to pay for specific treatments and doctors are paid on the basis of the procedures that they actually perform. This has the advantage of only paying doctors for the work they do and, in crude terms, of rewarding most heavily those who do the most work. It can also give doctors some freedom in terms of deciding how they want to balance their workload and reward those who respond best to patient demand. However, there are considerable disadvantages, including difficulties for the government in planning annual budgets in advance and the danger that doctors will be incentivised to prescribe more than is necessary or to offer treatments with higher rates even when there are reasonable alternatives that carry lower rates.

Finally, there is the option of using a *capitation payment system*, in which doctors are simply paid a fixed amount for each patient registered with their practice. This approach offers something of a balance between the other two, rewarding more popular or heavily worked practices with higher payments, but without creating incentives to increase treatment levels or utilise the most expensive procedures. Nevertheless, there are risks that doctors may take on more patients than they can reasonably manage in such systems. In addition, if payments do not reflect the increased workload that might be attached to some patient groups (eg older people), there may be a risk that doctors will have incentives to push such patients towards alternative providers.

As each of these approaches carries advantages and disadvantages, some countries try to combine two or three of them, for instance, by offering a basic salary that is topped up by fee-for-service or capitation payments.

Key policy issues

Earlier in this chapter, we noted that healthcare provision is a subject of intense political debate in all countries. This is in no small part a consequence of the difficult balancing act that governments face in reconciling the very large demand for healthcare services with the need to place some limits on the very large costs of healthcare. With public spending budgets increasingly squeezed in recent decades, the issues of cost containment, value for money and service efficiency have unsurprisingly risen up the health policy agenda. Although the strategies deployed by governments have varied, commonly exercised approaches have included:

- the *tighter regulation and control* of medical practice, particularly in terms of recommending which treatments offer the best value for money;

- a related trend of *stronger management* of healthcare services (and, typically, an attempt to reduce the power of healthcare professionals to determine patterns of service provision in order to facilitate this);

- *increased one-off payments* from public service users (sometimes dubbed 'co-payments');

- *increased incentives* – usually in terms of tax breaks – for citizens to join private health insurance schemes in order to 'ease pressure' on public services; and

- injecting *greater competition* into public health services – by allowing public funds to be used to pay for private services and/ or encouraging public hospitals or health centres to compete with each other – in the hope that competition for patients will drive down costs.

We should stress that these cost-containment measures have not always been about reducing costs per se; indeed, many countries have continued to see their health budgets rise. Yet, many governments have undoubtedly tried to place a tighter grip on healthcare expenditures.

While guaranteeing value for money makes sense, the kinds of cost-containment strategies noted earlier do not come without consequences. Most notably, perhaps, attempts to increase the private part of the public–private mix of healthcare provision often increase the inequality of access to healthcare. As we noted in the previous section, the major incentive for joining a private health insurance scheme is usually that it offers service on more favourable terms: quicker treatment or access to the newest clinical procedures, for instance. Yet, because the costs of insurance are often out of reach for many people – either because their incomes are too low or because their poor healthcare status results in large premiums being quoted to them – greater use of private financing mechanisms will almost inevitably give some better healthcare services than others. Worse still, perhaps, the market failures we referred to earlier are likely to persist too, for the most favourable terms are likely to be offered to those least likely to be ill and vice versa for the simple reason that insurers have strong incentives to attract customers that are likely to return a profit (a process economists sometimes dub 'cream skimming'). While such differences in access to goods and services may be tolerable with regard to luxury goods such as sports cars or flat-screen televisions, much deeper *moral questions* are invoked when access to the service in question is part of our basic human rights. These questions are particularly acute in low-income countries, where public provision is patchy and where, consequently, access to modest services for some is contrasted with a much higher level of service provision for richer citizens able to cover the costs of private care (see Box 5.2).

Yet, these hugely important concerns about equity of access and the fulfilment of human rights need to be balanced against the rights of citizens to spend their own money as they so wish. Indeed, just as there is a strong moral case for limiting inequalities in access to healthcare, if the state feels the need to limit healthcare provision – and rationing at some point is an inevitability – then there is also a strong moral claim for allowing citizens to use their own money to fund, say, potentially life-saving surgery that the government believes is too experimental to justify the use of public funds. Indeed, few governments now place such restrictions on their citizens. In high-income countries with well-established and extensive public health services, these tensions between containing the costs of public services, on the one hand, and trying to limit the inequities that arise from the widespread use of private alternatives by the better off, on the other, have arguably been exacerbated in recent years by the rising expectations of consumers and the ever-increasing scope of medical care as a consequence of technological and scientific advancement. In many of these countries, debate about the quality of services has intensified and, with governments unable to meet the full extent of demand for healthcare services, even nations with the best-funded services have witnessed an increase in the size of their private healthcare markets since the start of the 1980s. In Sweden, for instance, private healthcare expenditure accounted for just 7% of total healthcare spending in 1980, but by 2012, it had more than tripled to 23% of total health spending (OECD, 2014h).

In part, then, rising private expenditures are a response to the dilemmas of healthcare rationing. We noted earlier that all healthcare systems must exercise some form of rationing. The traditional response in social democratic systems has been to ration via waiting lists: when capacity is limited, patients will be added to a queue based on the urgency of their case and asked to wait (sometimes for many months) for their turn. Added to this, rationing has also increasingly taken place on the basis of publicly determined judgements about the effectiveness or value for money provided by specific interventions. In short, public systems need public gatekeepers – sometimes doctors, sometimes bureaucrats – who will restrict access to services. By contrast, private systems do not restrict access on the basis of such rules. Instead, rationing is determined by market conditions. If capacity is scare, then the price goes up and those who cannot afford treatment will miss out. It is important to note, therefore, that rising private expenditures do not resolve issues surrounding healthcare rationing, but merely allow some people to circumvent the queues or closed gates presented to them by public systems. Moreover, in predominantly private systems such as the US, we often find considerable numbers of people who have to go without healthcare because they are priced out of the market. Despite a major health reform in the US that took effect from 2010 onwards ('Obamacare'), more than 42 million Americans still had no health insurance in 2013 for instance (Smith and Medalia, 2014).

That said, we should again be wary of painting a one-sided picture here. While private expenditures have risen in many countries since the 1980s, in some countries, there is an intensive debate about how to extend the scale and scope of public provision. Since the beginning of the new millennium, for example, Malawi witnessed considerable increases – from 45% in 2000 to 75% in 2012 – in the share of health spending accounted for by public funds following considerable injections of additional finance (WHO, 2014). However, it is not just in low-income countries that we find examples like this. Some of the high-income countries noted for their relatively weak welfare states have increased their healthcare spending considerably in recent years. In the UK, for instance, one of the legacies of the Blair governments (1997–2007) was a considerable increase in the share of national income devoted to public expenditure on healthcare; at the same time, private spending remained stable at 19% of total healthcare during Blair's time in office – private healthcare expenditure as a share of total healthcare expenditure stood at roughly 17% in 2011 in the UK (Payne, 2013).

However, reform in the healthcare sector can often be slow-moving, not least because very strong external interests can counteract the will of governments. We noted at the start of the chapter that healthcare is big business in many countries. One consequence of this is that big businesses are usually keen to protect their business interests. Very large multinational pharmaceutical and medical supplies companies, for instance, work hard to ensure that their intellectual property rights are respected and that their profit margins are protected. In many countries, governments have become concerned about the rising costs of prescription medicines, but can find it tough to drive costs down because patent protections often restrict the production of a drug – particularly a new one – to the company that developed it. Similarly, private health insurance companies usually lobby to resist the expansion of state activity in healthcare for fear that it will encroach on their own business.

In all the fields of policy we consider in this book, there are many competing interests that continually use their influence to shape policy, but many political scientists have highlighted healthcare as a special case because of the relative *political strength of the medical profession* and the difficulties that this can create for governments looking to push through reforms that challenge the interests of the profession (Hudson and Lowe, 2009). This strength is evident both at the collective and the individual level, and both dimensions are worth briefly considering.

At the individual level, managers often find it very difficult to impose policy on individual clinicians. In large part, this is because the sheer complexity of many medical interventions makes it very difficult for non-medical specialists to observe, measure and understand the nuances of medical practice. Many attempts to increase the accountability of clinicians to managers by, for instance, using detailed computer-based accounting packages to track their work activity have struggled because such computer systems rely heavily on the medics themselves to provide information about their own work patterns; if doctors are unwilling to cooperate with the collection of data, then the systems are of limited use. Moreover, even if they are willing to cooperate, the collection of data can be a very time-consuming and costly exercise that diverts resources away from patient care. This is a problem that affects both public and private suppliers of healthcare. Indeed, if anything, it is a greater issue for private providers, for they need much more detailed data on activity in order to bill insurers and, equally, private insurers demand more detailed data in order to be sure that they are not being overcharged; this is reflected in the much higher administrative costs in private and more market-based public systems. Interestingly, cost-containment measures introduced in recent decades have often led to an increase in the number of managers in health systems and in overall administrative costs. While better management certainly holds the potential to deliver better value for money and, indeed, the more efficient delivery of healthcare services, in some countries, a backlash against this trend has resulted in attempts to reduce the number of managers in order to free up resources for front-line services.

At the collective level, medics are usually strongly represented by powerful professional associations that are well-respected and well-connected within government circles. In many countries, these organisations are consulted by the government as a matter of course when healthcare reforms are being considered and they are consequently well-placed to make the interests of the profession heard. While it certainly makes sense to consult the medical profession before making any radical changes to healthcare services, some have argued that the interests of the profession are heard too strongly and that health services too often serve the medical profession's interests at the expense of patient interests. Certainly, it is the case that medics are usually very well-paid and are often offered favourable terms of public practice that, for instance, allow them time to undertake private duties in addition to their publicly funded roles.

More generally, however, some sociologists have argued that health services might be better termed 'sickness services'. This critique suggests that, in part, because of the power of the medical profession, health policy is dominated by the so-called biomedical model of health. This model of healthcare emphasises clinical interventions that address illness and disease and can be contrasted with a social model of health, which emphasises the importance of broader environmental factors in shaping healthcare outcomes. Indeed, one of the major ironies of health policy is that once reasonable service levels have been established for all, it becomes difficult to establish a link between increased levels of expenditure on medical services and improved healthcare outcomes, such as life expectancy or infant mortality. Indeed, despite having the highest level of healthcare spending in the world, the US actually has a lower level of life expectancy than virtually every Western European country (see Figure 5.2). Some have even argued that the biggest health outcome gains have resulted from public health measures that do not rely on medical intervention: removing impurities from water supplies, improving levels of nutrition or making the use of seatbelts in cars compulsory, for instance (McKeown, 1979). Yet, funding for these measures is minimal compared with funding for medical interventions, perhaps, in part, because the political emphasis is firmly on the biomedical model in most countries.

Although we should be very wary of denigrating the huge value of effective medical interventions, the importance of a broader social understanding of healthcare becomes clear when we consider health inequalities within nations. In many countries, there are often stark contrasts in, for instance, the life expectancy of people with different income levels: in 2014, the life expectancy of males with the lowest incomes in the UK was about 10 years shorter than that for males with the highest earnings, while women on higher earnings expected to live seven years longer than those on the lowest earnings (ONS, 2014). Moreover, because income inequalities often interact with other social divisions, there are sometimes equally stark differences between different groups of people. In Australia, for instance, an Aboriginal or Torres Straits Islander male born in 2010–2012 had a life expectancy of just 69 years, about a decade shorter than the 79.7 years that a non-indigenous male could expect; the life expectancies

Figure 5.2: Life expectancy[a] and income inequality[b]

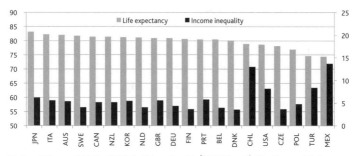

Notes: [a] Years at birth, 2012 (left-hand axis). [b] 80/20 quintile disposable income share, 2012 (right-hand axis).

Source: OECD.stat.

for Aboriginal or Torres Straits Islander and non-indigenous females were 73.7 and 83.1 years, respectively (ABS, 2013). These major differences in life chances are fundamentally shaped by broad social inequalities in societies – particularly the quality of living and working environments – and cannot be mitigated by medical services alone. Moreover, in some nations, these inequalities are reinforced by the healthcare system itself. Returning to the US, for example, in 2013, 9.8% of non-Hispanic white people did not have health insurance coverage, compared with 15.9% of black people and 24.3% of Hispanic people (Smith and Medalia, 2014).

What this points to is that healthcare outcomes, healthcare systems and broader social and environmental factors are heavily interlinked. Indeed, the so-called 'biopsychosocial model of health' recognises that our physical, mental and social well-being are heavily related and promotes a much broader perspective of healthcare. Although we have focused primarily on medical services here in order to constrain the scope of our chapter, it is important that the broad links between health policy and other key pillars, such as housing, social security and social care, are not forgotten. In fact, some would argue that income inequality is a key determinant of various health outcomes (see Figure 5.2). Joining up healthcare services with other key pillars of welfare is therefore one of the major challenges facing policy makers.

KEY POINTS SUMMARY

- ■ Healthcare is one of the largest items of public spending.
- ■ Healthcare systems almost always involve a complex mixed economy of public and private provision and funding.
- ■ All health services ration the supply of healthcare in order to cope with the pressures of demand.
- ■ Levels of demand for health services are rising, not least because of technological and demographic change.
- ■ Most countries' health policies have shown a greater concern with cost-containment measures in recent years.
- ■ All healthcare systems have some inequalities of access and the structure of those systems can contribute to inequalities.
- ■ Healthcare outcomes are fundamentally shaped by underlying social and economic inequalities.
- ■ Governments face unusually strong political interests in the arena of health policy and this can present difficulties for policy making and for the management of health services.

KEY READING GUIDE

Baggott (2012), Pascall (2012) and Alcock et al (2008: ch 12) all provide comprehensive introductory discussions of health and health care in the UK and beyond. Hill and Irving (2009: ch 7) and Powell (2014) provide excellent accounts of the historical origins of the NHS, as well as recent healthcare policy responses by UK governments in order to meet its most pressing challenges. Blakemore and Warwick-Booth's (2013: ch 8) discussion will be particularly interesting for those wanting to learn about the role of the medical profession in healthcare provision, while Glasby and Daly (2014) put an emphasis on current challenges in adult and social care (see also Chapter 7, this volume).

An excellent and long-standing introductory text is Ham's (2004) *Health policy in Britain*; Baggott's (2007) *Understanding health policy* and Hunter et al's (2010) *The public health system in England* are very useful too. All of these texts focus mainly on the British case, however; Blank and Burau (2013) provide a more international perspective. Donaldson (2011) offers an accessible health economist's view on the fiscal future of healthcare, while Nettleton's (2006) *The sociology of health and illness* provides a very good overview of the medical sociology literature. Glennerster (2003) also offers a guide to issues surrounding the financing of healthcare. Finally, Smith (2003) and Asthana and Halliday (2006) provide an extensive discussion of healthcare inequalities and what can be done to tackle them.

The OECD provides a lot of easily accessible information about healthcare systems and healthcare spending on its website (available at: www.oecd.org). Its OECD Health Data (see OCED, 2014h) package is particularly useful and provides data on a wide range of healthcare-related activities. The United Nations Development Programme (UNDP) provides data on a smaller range of indicators but for a much larger set of countries as part of its Human Development Report series (see: http://hdr.undp.org/en). The World Health Organisation provides a lot of data via its website too, including access to the World Health Organisation Statistical Information System (WHOSIS) (see: www.who.int/whosis/en/).

6

housing

Introduction

In terms of people's welfare and well-being, having a roof over their heads – housing – is hard to beat in terms of significance. Article 25 of the Universal Declaration of Human Rights (United Nations General Assembly, 1948) lists housing as being an essential right necessary for people's health and well-being and Article 12 notes that the home is a private sanctuary in which citizens must be free from undue interference of their privacy. The home is typically the focal point of family life.

Housing policy is naturally, therefore, a major concern of governments. However, it is often suggested that housing differs from the other pillars of welfare that we have examined in this book so far because such a high proportion of it is supplied and distributed through the private sector. Indeed, in most countries, it is common to talk of the 'housing market' rather than a housing service because it is usual for between 60% and 80% of housing to be supplied through the private market, either as rental properties managed by private landlords or as privately owned homes that are bought and sold by individuals (see Figure 6.1). Even in societies with a high proportion of state-owned housing or where the state strongly regulates the private rental part of the housing market (such as in France and Sweden), home-ownership and private landlords together make up the majority of housing provision. In addition, the vast majority of housing – whether state or market – is *built* by private construction companies.

Housing also differs from key areas of the welfare state in so far as a high proportion of the resources expended in the area comes in the form of capital expenditure on 'bricks and mortar' and the purchase of building land. Many other pillars of welfare – education, healthcare and employment training, for example – are primarily *services* delivered to people, and are very labour-intensive rather than capital-intensive, or, as with the case of social security, are focused on recurrent cash transfers rather than long-term investments.

In other chapters, we have tried to give an indication of the scale of the size of each pillar by referring to the overall level of government spending in the sector; as will become clear during the course of this chapter, it is difficult to provide equivalent figures for housing because spending is haphazard and spread across many different functions and, moreover, because government policy often aims to influence activity in the private sphere without directly controlling it. Indeed, housing has been described as 'the *wobbly pillar* under the welfare state' because of these features and much of the welfare state literature mistakenly downplays housing because of its reliance on the open market. It is important at the outset to realise that, despite this, housing is still a major pillar with which the state is closely concerned.

It is also important to note that the concept of 'the home' has what are often deep cultural roots in each nation – the very words 'home' and 'housing' conjure up mental images that delve deeply into our psyche (see Box 6.1). Yet, those images may vary vastly from nation to nation, be it in terms of the style of the typical home, its size, the standard of amenities that might be expected within the home, the number of people who typically occupy the household or who is likely to own the property. What is more, while the home is a place of security and belonging for many, housing is often insecure and the home can be a place of nightmares. Homelessness is a major social problem in many countries and results in people being separated from the normal securities and comforts of a home (Lowe, 2004).

Box 6.1: The concept of 'home'

The idea of home is universally and instinctively understood. People who have lived abroad talk about 'coming home'. We intuitively think of home in relation to the wider world 'out there' beyond our front doors. The concept is closely bound up with creating our own self-identity – where we are most 'ourselves'. The sociologist Giddens (1991) suggests that the home is the main place where social life is sustained and, above all, reproduced. The French sociologist Bachelard (1992) believed that the home was critical to our deepest psychic well-being and that rooms, pieces of furniture, nooks and crannies in the house – how they smell, their echoes and their secret memories – make the home a sanctuary; as he says, 'the house allows one to dream in peace' (Bachelard, 1992: 4).

A good example of the idea of home in practice is the idea of domesticity, which was invented in 19th-century England. Victorian domestic culture was imbued with a sense of the home as a retreat from a hostile world outside. This powerful culture, with its strong moral purpose, spread across the British Empire and took root in all the English-speaking nations. Throughout the 20th century, interest in the domestic interior persisted and found expression in the obsession with home decoration and the 'makeover' of rooms and gardens, as seen in numerous television programmes. This sense of being acceptably fashionable is not a new idea and is a contemporary expression of conformity through home-making.

In the 21st century, the digital revolution and the invention of the Internet have transformed how people's homes are used, with an increase in 'home-working', new types of leisure activity (eg home-cinema) and new relationships with commercial organisations (eg home-banking). In an era of globalisation, when we all reside on a planet where time and space have new meanings, it is clear that the home is ever-more important to people's social and psychological well-being.

Key policy goals

As our introduction should make clear, while housing is a very personal and, in many ways, private issue, housing is also of great concern to the state in terms of a number of fundamental policy issues. Chief among the concerns of the government is the need to ensure that there is an adequate supply of housing. Changing population levels, increased life expectancy, changing family formations, migration, the movement of people in and out of different regions of a nation or even in and out of different parts of a town or city all create challenges in terms of housing supply. A vital part of housing policy is to try to match the quantity of homes in any given area with the number that need to be supplied in relation to the current and forecast number of households.

Added to this, changing lifestyles and family forms require the government not only to plan supply on the basis of the number of homes needed, but also to think about the type and size of properties that are needed to meet the needs of modern family types. Fluctuating birthrates, life expectancy, marriage rates and divorce rates can all influence the demand for different sizes and designs of property; for example, bungalows and city-centre flats will likely appeal to different groups of people. Changing economic fortunes or consumer expectations, even changing fashions, also have a role to play in influencing the level of demand for different types of housing (Bramley et al, 2004).

Closely linked to the issue of the size and type of properties are issues surrounding the standard of housing. As we noted in other chapters, the quality of housing fundamentally influences healthcare outcomes and well-being more generally. In addition, living in poor-quality housing is often an outcome of income-related poverty and can contribute towards social exclusion. Improving the standard of housing, therefore, can be important not only as a goal of housing policy, but also in addressing broader social policy issues.

Finally, and on a related note, the affordability of housing is a crucial issue. High housing costs can create major social problems, be it in terms of contributing to income poverty by stretching household budgets to their limits, reducing the flexibility of employment markets by presenting barriers to the movement of labour across a country, limiting family formation by restricting the size of families beyond that desired or, more simply, preventing people from leading a happy life because of the stresses of being unable to find affordable housing near to friends, family or work

How governments meet these policy goals varies somewhat from country to country. We will deal with the key policy mechanisms in more detail in the next section, but, in general terms, it is possible to divide most high-income nations into one of two broad housing systems.

Figure 6.1: Market^a versus non-market housing^b

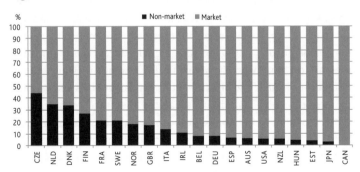

Notes: ^a Percentage of dwelling stock that is owner-occupied or privately rented, 2009
^b Percentage of dwelling stock that is not owner-occupied or privately rented, 2009

Source: OECD.stat

First, there are home-owning-dominated societies in which the majority of houses are private properties owned by individual citizens (see Figure 6.1). In such systems, the housing market often acts as an important driver of the economy, with housing being a major focus of personal investment, and a key role of the state is to ensure the smooth running of the market and to stimulate its growth. However, the costs of purchasing houses are such that not everyone will be able to afford to own their own home or, indeed, will want to, so a significant proportion of the population will still rent homes. In such systems, there is typically a clear separation between public and private renting. Private renting is usually unsubsidised and fully commercial in pricing, effectively an adjunct of the home-ownership market, with private property-owners free to buy, sell or rent their properties with relatively few restrictions. Public renting, meanwhile, is typically a residual state-run safety net for low-income households, with rents subsidised by the state in order to keep them low or even to cover the cost entirely for some households. In addition, the state often supports those on low incomes via indirect subsidies for private renting in the form of housing allowances paid through the social security system (see Chapter 2). This type of housing system is typical of the high-income English-speaking nations, such as the UK, the US and Australia (Kemeny, 2005).

By contrast, the second type of housing system that some countries operate is the mixed/plural system, in which there is a more balanced approach. Here, owner-occupation remains an important part of the overall picture, but is not such a driving force, and there is less pressure on those who can afford to do so to buy their own home. Instead, both public and private renting play larger roles and although the two sectors are again clearly separated, they usually operate in the context of a more harmonised rent-setting system that is overseen by local authorities. This regulation of rents is one of the factors that gives renting a broader appeal in these countries. In other words, the market is more heavily constrained in these systems and the state's role extends beyond that of provider of residual housing as a supplement to a favoured private market. This system is commonly found in Northern and Western Europe (see Figure 6.2).

Figure 6.2: Size of rental market[a]

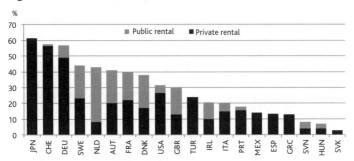

Note: [a] Percentage of dwelling stock privately or publicly rented, 2009.

Source: OECD.stat.

There used to be a third approach, state-led housing, in which the government took the lead role in building, allocating and maintaining housing. Here, the role of the private market was heavily constrained and, sometimes, in principle eliminated. What this meant in practice was that the state allocated and reallocated property and so the market mechanism was replaced with a bureaucratic approach (Lowe and Tsenkova, 2003). This also meant that there was little in the way of commercial construction, with house-building largely undertaken by the state; families who were outside the state sector had no alternative other than to build their own home. This state-led approach almost completely disappeared following the collapse of the communist bloc in Eastern and Central Europe (see Box 6.2) and was not found in high-income countries at all; however, it still broadly characterises the housing system in Cuba, for instance, although recent reforms have begun to significantly expand private ownership even here.

In each of these systems of housing, the state plays an important role, but it differs widely from that of market regulator and provider of last-resort safety net through to main provider. Likewise, the role of the private market varies too, from dominant provider, through restricted provider to minority player. Significantly, these differing roles for the state and the market usually reflect differing values and goals with regard to the role of the housing market. While, in essence, in home-owning-dominated systems, the market is left to operate relatively freely because it is viewed as an important source of wealth and asset accumulation, in other systems, stronger restrictions are placed on the market in order to emphasise *broader social concerns* surrounding housing affordability.

Box 6.2: Post-communist housing

One of the most dramatic political changes in recent years was the collapse of the Union of Soviet Socialist Republics (USSR) and the other European communist states. Under the communist system, a large share of housing production was organised and managed by the state. There were, however, considerable variations in the balance of state and private housing. For example, in Hungary, nearly 80% of new housing between 1946 and 1990 was self-built (private building firms were not allowed) – people used their own resources and labour. Housing was used as an incentive to ensure that key workers – doctors, teachers, engineers and so on – moved to where they were needed. Generally, the state provided housing at very low costs and cheap food, but in a very low-wage economy. In fact, housing was traded on a massive scale through a black market of cash and 'hard currency' deals. Most rural housing in all these countries was and remained owner-occupied.

When communism collapsed in Central and Eastern Europe at the end of the 1980s, most of the economies were bankrupt and state flats were sold simply because local governments could not afford to manage and maintain them. Selling state flats at low prices was also a 'shock absorber' for the dramatic changes to these economies that were taking place as they adjusted to global market prices. As private renting had been virtually abolished under communism, and because most state rental flats were sold, these countries have become 'super-owner-occupied'. Countries such as Estonia, Hungary and Slovakia have home-owning rates in excess of 90% of households (see Figure 6.3). Other nations have retained some of their rental stock but the emphasis has mostly been on rapid privatisation.

The economy of China has also been liberalised since 1978, although the country remains a socialist state. A policy for the gradual privatisation of housing has also been followed, in parallel with the European post-communist nations. State flats have been progressively sold off and an open property market has developed rapidly alongside the marketisation of the wider Chinese economy. Indeed, such has been the pace of change that privately owned housing is now dominant and housing affordability has become a major policy issue.

Indeed, home-ownership has come to dominate housing in many post-communist societies, producing a new variety of housing system, and it remains to be seen what the wider impact on society and the emerging welfare states will be in these countries.

Key delivery mechanisms

As we have already made clear, all housing systems involve some mix of publicly and privately owned properties and, in addition, a distinction can be drawn between those who own their own home ('owner-occupiers') and those who rent their home. Owning and renting are the two principal forms of housing tenure. The idea of 'tenure' arises because housing is lived in (consumed) by private individual households behind their own front doors. This is a key difference between housing and other welfare pillars such as health and education because they are mainly services provided in a collective setting – a hospital ward, a school classroom and so on. The word 'tenure' comes from the Latin verb *tenere*, which means 'to hold', and tenure indicates who has possession of a property.

Owner-occupiers either own their home (and the land on which it is built) outright or are in the process of buying it using a special form of loan called a mortgage. Strong property rights are a feature of most democracies and, as a consequence, homeowners have considerable autonomy in the running of their homes and it is difficult to remove someone's right to occupy the property as a consequence. This provides considerable security for homeowners but also creates rigidity in the housing market. Property-ownership can also provide individuals with a valuable asset that acts as an important form of wealth accumulation. Set against this, owner-occupiers are responsible for the upkeep of their property and can be exposed to considerable financial risk as a consequence. Similarly, if an owner-occupier is in the process of paying a mortgage on a property, then a failure to meet repayments on that loan can lead to them losing this property to the lender.

Those who rent their rooms, flat or house from a landlord who owns the property are known as tenants. Landlords come in many forms and can be the state, a private individual, a company or a non-governmental organisation. For tenants, the payment of a weekly rent to the landlord gives the tenant legal occupation of the dwelling in a package of rights and responsibilities. The advantage of renting over ownership is that tenants do not have to worry about the basic maintenance of the property and it is much easier and cheaper to move elsewhere should the property no longer be suitable.

A third, but much less common, form of tenure in some countries is that of leaseholder. This form of tenure usually exists when one large building is split into multiple properties: a block of flats, for example. In such instances, a distinction can be drawn between the freeholder – who owns the building as a whole in perpetuity – and the individual leaseholders who buy long-term leases (99 years is common), which give them ownership of, say, one of the flats in the apartment block. Typically, the leaseholder has responsibility for the upkeep of the internal aspects of their property, while the freeholder is responsible for communal areas (eg stairways, corridors) and the fabric of the building itself.

Although there is a specific legal package of rights and responsibilities associated with each of the principal tenures, they are not in strict law always as different from each other as might be imagined. In some countries, tenancy rights are so secure that they amount to control over the property normally associated with ownership. For example, the tenancy can be inherited by family members. In most legal systems around the world, a tenancy agreement means that the owner of the property (the landlord) gives up their right of possession for the period of the tenancy, although many private landlords often imagine that it is still 'theirs' and find it hard to accept that the house or flat is out of their control.

Irrespective of the tenure of a property, the physical manifestation of housing provides a distinctive feature of this pillar of welfare. Much of the expenditure in the housing field comes during the construction of a property and, once it is built, it cannot be moved. All of these factors mean that considerable effort needs to go into the management and maintenance of the existing housing stock. The relatively fixed nature of housing – particularly when privately owned – needs to be stressed here. It is the existence of historical housing that marks housing as a little different from the other welfare state pillars. Housing is fixed and durable and the stock is added to very slowly; typically less than 1% of new housing is added per annum in high-income countries As a result, housing is usually (although not always) much slower to change than the other areas of social policy and many housing problems arise from this historical legacy.

Running in parallel to these four stages is the crucial issue of *housing finance*. Housing production is very expensive compared to average household income. As a result, governments often have to have regard not only to whether a sufficient quantity of housing is being built, but also to whether the 'consumers' (owners and tenants alike) can afford to pay the often high costs of housing.

As we noted earlier, most owner-occupiers have bought or are in the process of buying their home. As the cost of a house or flat can typically be anything between three and 10 times the size of annual household incomes, some mechanism is needed to spread out the costs over a long period of time. This is done in the form of long loans called mortgages, in which credit is paid back over a period usually ranging from 15 to 30 years but with a large amount of interest on the outstanding debt. Here, in broad terms, the property and the loan are tied together, with the lender (usually a bank) retaining the title deeds that assign legal ownership of the property until the full extent of the loan is paid off. Crucially, the terms of the contract signed when a mortgage is arranged allow for the lender to repossess the property if the household cannot afford the repayments on the loan. This entails the lender retaking ownership of the property and then selling it in order to get their money back. Obviously, repossession is an extremely stressful event and, in some countries, governments offer financial support to owner-occupiers who risk losing their home as a consequence of a change in their financial status.

If all goes well, an owner-occupier's home is not only a place to live, but can also be a considerable financial asset. Most owner-occupiers have considerable equity in their house – the difference between the current market value of the house and what they owe any lender on a mortgage – and can borrow against this equity to release capital for other purposes. Often, such borrowing funds private welfare consumption such as the payment of a child's school or university fees or the funding of one-off medical interventions. Similarly, for many homeowners, their house forms an important part of their overall investment plans for retirement, with many moving to smaller/cheaper houses later in life and using the surplus equity they release by doing so to supplement pensions or cover the costs of care (Lowe, 2004).

Owner-occupation may sometimes seem like a private matter that has little to do with the government, but this is not so. Even in countries in which home-owning dominates, the state still plays a strong role in regulating housing standards and in controlling how properties can be modified through planning laws. In addition, some countries provide tax subsidies to those purchasing property (eg by allowing mortgage interest payments to be offset against income tax payments) or similar incentive schemes. Conversely, it is sometimes the case that when countries offer welfare services on a means-tested basis, the value of property is taken into account as part of an asset test, meaning that those with property of considerable value may be excluded from receiving state funding for particular services. More generally, the state also oversees the housing property market and plays a huge role in terms of promoting its stability and smooth running. In particular, its economic policies play a huge role in influencing the cost of mortgage repayments because, in most countries, the government either sets interest rates directly or has considerable influence over the independent central banks that do so.

Although tenants themselves do not have the long-term commitment of a mortgage, they still play an important role in the housing finance market because their rent goes to a landlord who has to pay a mortgage (or who makes a large profit if the debt has been paid off). One of the disadvantages of renting is that tenants never own the equity of the property – even if they have lived in it their entire adult life – and, indeed, the fruits of the investment they have largely funded go entirely to the landlord. Moreover, not only do tenants miss out on these capital gains, but they also pay rent continuously for their whole life rather than paying towards a mortgage for a fixed period.

Given the often high costs of housing and the considerable wealth that can be tied to privately owned property, housing can fundamentally influence the distribution of wealth and income and heavily shape income poverty and income inequality. Consequently, most countries put in place mechanisms for addressing potential imbalances arising from this division in the housing market.

On the one hand, as we have noted earlier, in many countries, governments subsidise rent levels by: offering social rented housing to those on low incomes at sub-market rates; regulating the rents that can be charged by private landlords in order to ensure a broad degree of affordability or fairness; or by offering housing allowances to low-income households via the social security system. In terms of the latter, some countries offer dedicated payments (eg at the time of writing, the UK has a specific 'housing benefit'), while others include such payments as part of regular unemployment benefit payments or pension payments, for instance.

On the other hand, most governments also tax the capital gains accrued from privately owned property. Mechanisms for doing this include levying charges on profits when a landlord sells a property that was not their primary home and taxing income raised from property rents. In addition, most countries have some form of inheritance tax that places a charge on estates when a property-owner dies; these taxes play an important role in rebalancing wealth within nations, for the transfer of property assets from one generation to the next heavily reinforces income differentials between social classes.

A more radical strategy to address divides between property-owners and renters that some governments have adopted has been to allow those in rented public housing to buy their house from the state at a heavily discounted rate. These privatisations of public housing are usually part of a concerted policy effort to increase home-ownership rates. In terms of easing the move towards home-ownership, some countries have also implemented programmes that offer financial assistance (usually in the form of a subsidised loan) to key public sector workers for whom the cost of housing is out of reach, and, similarly, some governments use planning laws to place pressure on developers to include some affordable housing in any major new property developments.

While many of these mechanisms aim to address questions of housing affordability, homelessness is an issue in all societies (see Box 6.3). The bottom line here is that in every society, problems arise because there is not enough property at a price that people can afford or simply because there is an insufficient supply. Overcrowded houses, rough sleepers on the streets, housing in poor physical shape and excessively high house prices are all symptoms that there is something wrong in the balance of households to dwellings. It is the aim of most governments to try to promote the sufficient supply of an adequate standard of housing. What is deemed an adequate standard depends very much on the wider economic health of particular nations. What is then done about implementing the standard varies considerably according to the policy direction taken by governments of different political persuasions. As a general rule, governments try to advance housing standards in line with economic growth.

How a particular nation responds to housing shortages also depends on circumstances that are often beyond its control. For example, almost all the nations of Western and Central Europe suffered dramatic setbacks in their housing programmes as a result of the First and Second World Wars during the 20th century, a combined total of over 10 years when almost no housing was built, there was considerable destruction of civilian property and demand from new households soared. In Britain, for example, the Second World War created a deficit of households to dwellings of nearly 2 million by 1945 in a housing stock of only 12.5 million (Holmans, 2000). It was this level of massive deficit that was the context for post-war housing policy in almost every European nation and was one of the contributory factors in the widespread deployment of easy-to-build, prefabricated, concrete, high-rise tower blocks.

Moreover, housing shortages do not arise solely as a consequence of dramatic shocks that damage housing stock, such as war or earthquakes. Housing shortages typically arise because of more gradual changes in the population and lifestyles. Indeed, an important feature of the issue of the balance of households to dwellings is the fact that in high-income societies, the number of households grows faster than the population due to improvements in life expectancy and incomes. Put simply, when the number of adults in the population increases, this results in a larger pool of people potentially wanting to form a household. Added to this, other basic demographic changes can be significant. For example, in many countries, there has been a rapid growth in the number of single-person households. In Europe, this tendency began during the Second World War, with an increase in the number of widows, but it is now primarily a product of increasing divorce rates and, to a lesser extent, a rise in the number of people who make a lifestyle choice to live alone. All these changes mean that there is an increasing number of households relative to the size of the population. Strategic planning on the basis of population forecasts is therefore an important component of housing policy.

Box 6.3: Homelessness

Homelessness is a more complex state than is commonly understood. The European Observatory on Homelessness (see Edgar and Meert, 2006) has suggested a four-way definition that captures different types of homelessness well:

- **Rooflessness**: defined as being without any kind of shelter for all or most of the day. This includes people sleeping rough or having access only to a night shelter.
- **Houselessness**: defined as having a temporary place to stay in an institution or shelter. This includes people living in a hostel for the homeless, temporary accommodation for those recently released from prison but with no other fixed address or a reception centre for recently arrived migrants.
- **Living in insecure housing**: defined as those with insecure tenancies or unsafe housing. This includes people renting properties without proper legal contracts to secure their tenancy, those staying temporarily with friends or family, people occupying housing from which they are soon to be evicted (eg for non-payment of rents) and those whose housing is unsafe because of the threat of domestic violence.
- **Living in inadequate housing**: defined as those living in unfit or illegal housing. This includes people living in caravans that are not on legal sites, anyone living in makeshift housing, people living in extremely overcrowded housing and those in houses that fail to meet legal safety standards.

This classification not only usefully breaks homelessness down into a series of discrete but rather different subcategories, but also highlights well the link between homelessness and the concept of the home (see Box 6.1).

From an empirical viewpoint, the classification also allows for a more nuanced measurement of the nature and extent of homelessness. For example, a 2006 report that used this classification noted that there were an estimated 5,080 rough sleepers in France, but that there were also 46,469 living in homelessness hostels, an estimated 150,000 living temporarily with family or friends, some 2,000 living in illegal buildings, 103,285 living under the threat of eviction, 1,150,000 living in unfit housing and 1,037,000 living in overcrowded housing (Edgar and Meert, 2006). However, this definition is far from exhaustive; indeed, the European Observatory on Homelessness has itself suggested a still more detailed definition in its recent work (Edgar, 2009).

Key policy issues

As is no doubt evident by now, housing is a complex field of social policy in which the state has to balance a wide range of public and private concerns. In so doing, it is faced with numerous policy dilemmas, and the often slow-moving nature of housing change can make it difficult to rapidly reshape the nature of housing provision.

Indeed, the housing stock in any nation consists of all the accumulated dwellings built in the past, representing many different styles of building, designs and building programmes. Each nation's own specific history will have a profound impact on its housing stock. For example, as we have noted, in most European countries after the Second World War, a high proportion of new housing was built in the form of high-rise blocks of flats that, quite literally, had a towering impact on the urban landscape that persists today in many places. In recent years, some of the biggest of these have been blown up in some countries because they were regarded as undesirable and became associated with social problems. However, in other cities – such as Stockholm, Budapest and Vienna – high-rise flats have a long tradition and have not been viewed in a negative light. In the UK, the effects of its very early industrialisation and consequent urbanisation are still felt today in its housing stock: a very high proportion of the housing in its major cities is old, with more than a quarter being built in the 19th century despite subsequent slum clearance programmes and extensive bomb damage during the Blitz in the Second World War. Indeed, around a third of dwellings in the UK were built before 1945 and the same is true of some neighbouring countries, including Denmark, France and Italy. In many European countries, older housing (often located in the most central neighbourhoods because of its age) is often among the most prized and expensive housing, whereas in many parts of East Asia, 'used' housing is often less highly prized than newly built houses.

However, while housing stock generally changes rather slowly, the financial instruments surrounding housing have changed rapidly in recent decades. What has most strikingly changed is the rise of so-called 'weightless' financial trading, which has enabled vast flows of globally sourced capital to flow round the planet and the evolution of a truly global mortgage market in which geographical boundaries have come to mean very little. The key issue here is that this process has given rise to the expansion of home-ownership in many countries (for rates in 2009, see Figure 6.3; see also the interactive app version for historical data), as well as rising house prices in many countries.

This change in private financing has impacted on welfare states in important ways. Without being able to provide detail here, across almost all the Organisation for Economic Co-operation and Development (OECD) nations, very low interest rates available across the world financial markets enabled a widening spectrum of people to buy property. Huge amounts of capital were made available for lending, especially in the US housing market, through a new process in which individual mortgages were packaged together and sold as bonds into the global financial system. These bonds were bought by pension funds, life insurance companies and other investors who needed to hold *long-term* investments. As families pay back their mortgages over 20 or 25 years, so these bonds became more and more valuable, turning debts into capital. Some of these bundled-up mortgages turned out to have been mis-sold by mortgage brokers in the US, leading to many low-income families defaulting on their payments, meaning that these bonds, in turn, were not as valuable as they at first appeared; indeed, some of them were positively 'toxic'. The scale of this problem was huge and was one of the reasons for the crisis in the financial markets in 2007/08

Figure 6.3: Home ownership rates[a]

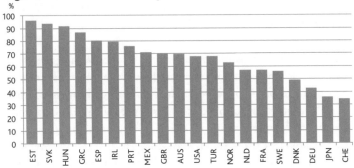

Note: [a] Percentage of dwelling stock owner-occupied, 2009.

Source: OECD.stat.

and the global financial crisis that followed. This crisis, in turn, resulted in major cutbacks in public spending taking place in many countries.

However, for at least three decades before the crisis, homeowners saw the value of their property increase rapidly as people scrambled to get on the property ladder. Over time, families discovered that their homes were very valuable indeed – worth much more than they were originally bought for, even discounting the mortgage. This 'housing equity' was, in effect, a store of wealth that was accessible by remortgaging (taking out a new low-interest loan), so enabling families to advance their spending plans. Evidence is gathering that the ability to unlock housing equity in this way has change the way people think about their home in many countries. It has become more 'financialised'. There is evidence that the attitudes of families to the welfare state and their own welfare needs have been changed because of this new resource. For example, a study by Smith and Searle (2010), appropriately called 'Banking on housing', found that homeowners of all ages used housing equity usually at a time of family crisis – divorcing, unemployment, the birth of a child – and also accessed private services such as schooling, healthcare and so on using this equity. This process has been dubbed 'asset-based welfare' and is a real challenge to traditional ways of thinking about the welfare state. Homeowners can transfer between the public and private sectors at will and as a need or crisis arrives, people seeing their home as a financial 'cushion', a 'shield' or a 'blanket' in times of need.

Asset-based welfare is notably a feature of some welfare systems in East Asia. In Singapore, for example, the state more or less compels its citizens to build up individual funds through its Provident Savings scheme, being ready to spend as welfare needs arises. Housing assets are part and parcel of this fund; indeed, in Singapore, the government has required its citizens to buy state-built flats in high-rise apartment blocks using low-interest loans subsidised by the state. Private housing and the equity it stores is, as a result, at the core of the 'welfare state' of this country.

Another key issue that lies at the heart of welfare states, especially in Europe, is the connection between home-ownership and pensions. As homeowners gradually pay off their mortgages over 25 years or so, they often have low housing costs in older age (tenants, of course, have to keep paying rent to their landlord through the whole of their life). Some argue that differences in the balance of the size of the home-owning and rental sectors across countries therefore impact demands for pension provision. In home-owning societies, voters may accept lower levels of state pension because of their private assets, whereas in the countries that are in the 'mixed/plural' category, a higher level of pension income may be demanded. Indeed, Kemeny (2005) has argued that home-owning societies tend towards 'low-tax, low-spend' welfare states and the more rental-based nations tend towards 'high-tax, high-spend' welfare states.

In some of the home-owning countries, the division between owner-occupiers and renters has become a major problem. First, because tenants do not, of course, have access to housing equity, this impacts on their income and wealth, and in countries with targeted welfare systems, they are more likely to be state-dependent than home-owners. A second key issue that has emerged in many welfare states with high home-ownership rates is an intergenerational divide between better-off, older people (often having paid off their mortgages, so-called 'outright owners') who bought their home a long time ago and young professionals and young people generally simply because house prices have accelerated so rapidly *everywhere* that they are priced out.

Another social division arises from the fact that housing is 'locational': it exists in a particular place. In populous cities and, indeed, nations, social tensions often arise due to the demand for housing and other commercial interests to be located nearest high centres of population or near to central places with the best facilities and cultural amenities. Competition for space and competing uses is at the heart of major social tensions, with power plays between local communities and property developers often evident. Existing owners want to hang on to their advantages and keep at bay people who they may see as outsiders, and yet economic migrants, for example, may be essential to local economic vitality and progress. Right-wing and nationalist groups and political parties often campaign vociferously against Gypsies, Travellers, single parents, immigrants and asylum seekers, whom they regard as a threat to their property rights, jobs and well-being. The basic human instinct of a search for a settled home can become a tinderbox of political unrest. Almost all the great global cities of the world suffer from these issues of sustainable development and the reconciliation of seemingly incompatible interests. Quite often, it is the powerful and rich who win out by using their economic muscle and political connections to outmanoeuvre groups campaigning for the poor and powerless.

All of these issues and dilemmas of policy point, however, to the fact that 'housing' has become a central issue in how we need to think about and evaluate welfare state change and, indeed, the very nature and fabric of 21st-century society. In short, although housing is seen by some theorists as being at the margins of social policy, particularly in nations where owner-occupation dominates, such a view is flawed. Not only is access to housing central to our individual well-being, but the very nature of the housing system itself has an impact on how we live our lives, on how we plan for our futures, on our economies and, perhaps, on the very nature of welfare states.

KEY POINTS SUMMARY

■ The state has a major role to play in deciding how much housing needs to be built, what type and size of properties are needed, and the control of housing standards.

■ Creating a balance of households to dwellings is a fundamental aim of housing policy, but whether and/or how this is achieved varies according to a country's level of economic development and political traditions.

■ There are two main types of housing tenure – ownership and renting – and the balance of tenures in particular countries is critical to its housing system and also to the nature of the wider welfare state.

■ Housing differs from the other pillars of welfare because most activity and provision occurs in the private sector and a large part of the expenditure on housing is on the physical stock (capital), as contrasted to education or health, where continuing to deliver the service is the major cost.

■ Housing interacts with private finance in important ways, be it in allowing individuals to build up assets through home-ownership or, more widely, in underpinning the growth of global mortgage markets.

KEY READING GUIDE

Overviews of housing can be found in most core Social Policy textbooks. Particularly useful examples include: chapter 10 of *Understanding social policy* by Hill and Irving (2009) and chapter 16 of Bochel et al's (2009) *Social policy: themes, issues and debates*. Burnett (1986) and Holmans (1987) provide excellent historical accounts of the development of housing policy in the UK, one from the point of view of a social historian, the other written by an economist. Lowe (2011) offers an overview of recent developments, including detailed analysis of the global financial crisis. For students wanting to go to the next level in housing, this is the best available source. One of the best insights into the wider comparative focus is found in the work of Kemeny (1992, 2005).

The website of the independent research organisation the Joseph Rowntree Foundation is the gateway to many sources and contains short versions of the innumerable research studies that they have conducted (available at: www.jrf.org.uk). Similarly, a useful source in its own right but with many links to other sites is the Centre for Housing Policy at the University of York (see: www.york.ac.uk/chp/). At the European level, EUROSTAT (see: http://ec.europa.eu/eurostat) provides useful information on housing tenure and the European Federation of National Organisations Working with the Homeless (FEANTSA) runs the European Observatory on Homelessness, which provides data on the nature and extent of homelessness in Europe (see: www.feantsa.org/).

7

beyond the five pillars

Introduction

We have focused our attention in this *Short guide to social policy* on the traditional 'five giants' of social policy, but a fuller exploration of the subject matter would take us into a much broader array of policy areas. As we noted in Chapter 1, the value of a short guide comes in its ability to help the reader locate the major sights and sounds very quickly. However, we recognise that a short guide also carries risks: emphasising the major tourist sights may marginalise important landmarks that are off the traditional beaten path; providing context for a short tour might risk simplifying the complex realities of a place; or, worst of all, readers may restrict their tour to the main boulevards described in the guide and decline the invitation to explore further for themselves. In each chapter, we have offered guides to further reading when discussing the core pillars. These reading guides will help take you deeper into the detail of the pillars and into topic areas that extend beyond the core themes we have covered. In this chapter, we would like to broaden our focus a little by briefly highlighting some of the important sights and sounds that lie just outside the main boulevards we have described in the core of this book. We will do this by offering a very brief tour of three additional 'pillars' of social policy – which we loosely place under the headings of criminal justice, family policy and social care – before moving on to a still-broader reflection in the final chapter that points to a range of other key policy areas that we have been unable to give sustained attention to in our *Short guide to social policy*. We maintain the structure offered in the previous chapter in each policy area – examining key policy goals, key delivery mechanisms and key policy issues – but our discussion of each is necessarily much briefer than in the preceding chapters.

Family policy

Family policy: key policy goals

In recent years, 'family policy' has increasingly come to be seen as a distinctive area of social policy. This is not because separate provisions for families with children have not been a feature of the welfare state, far from it: family allowances (in this case, cash payments to families with more than one child) were a part of the UK's Beveridge reforms discussed in Chapter 1, for example. Instead, it reflects that there has been a growing concern in many countries, particularly high-income countries, with the pressures placed on families with children in modern economies. These include not only concerns with the additional costs of bringing up children, but also the challenges of balancing work and family life, particularly in the context of contemporary knowledge-based economies in which women are much more likely to participate in the labour market than was the case in the relatively recent past (see Chapter 3). Given that it is less commonly treated as a separate area of social policy than the 'five giants' explored in earlier chapters, there is less consensus over what falls under the domain of family policy, but it is typically deemed to include: family allowances, including benefits and tax credits; maternity and parental leave; childcare; birth-related services; and pre-school education.

This is a narrow definition of family policy and is rooted in a very narrow (and somewhat culturally specific) conception of the family as households with children. More expansive definitions would consider the family in a broader sense and might therefore expand the scope of policies so as to include care for older people, a topic that we address separately later when discussing social care. Some definitions of family policy would include interventions designed to shape the behaviour of families by, for example, trying to boost the stability of marriages, influencing parenting styles or, indeed, altering the perceived deviant and/or anti-social behaviours of members of a household. We briefly address some of these issues later when discussing criminal justice policy. This hints at overlaps with other areas of policy – especially social security policy, but others too – that complicate the discussion of family policy as a separate area.

Even when adopting the relatively narrow definition of family policy, we can observe major variations across countries in the level of family policy spending and in the overall goals of family policy. Figure 7.1 shows family policy spending as a percentage of gross domestic product (GDP) for 33 Organisation for Economic Co-operation and Development (OECD) countries in 2011. While for some countries, spending forms a large part of overall welfare state expenditure, in others, it is a relatively minor area of activity. So, for example, in Denmark, 4% of GDP was accounted for by family spending, almost double the level found in Germany (2.2%), just under three times the level in Greece or Spain (1.4%), and more than four times the level in the US (a mere 0.7% of GDP).

Figure 7.1: Family policy spending[a]

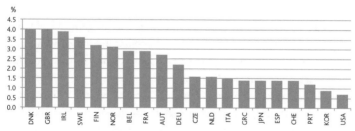

Note: [a] As a percentage of gross domestic product (GDP), 2011.

Source: OECD.stat.

However, levels of spending tell us little about the goals of spending, and for family policy, these are often informed by fundamental assumptions about the roles of men and women in society. Indeed, scholars have often drawn a distinction between family policy packages designed around a *traditional male-breadwinner family model* and those designed around a *dual-earner model*. In the traditional male-breadwinner model, policies maintain the traditional gender roles of men undertaking paid employment and women undertaking caring roles in the family. By contrast, in the dual-earner model, both men and women are encouraged to participate in the labour market, with family policies often being used to help families balance the challenges of working and caring for children. However, we can observe differences within the dual-earner model. While some countries aim to encourage a dual-earner labour market model *and* a greater role for men in caring duties, others demand greater female participation in the labour market while doing little to facilitate a more expansive role for men in caring work. In other words, to gain a full picture of the dual-earner model in each country, we need to consider not only the ways in which policy tries to facilitate growth in female labour market participation, but also the extent to which family policy supports and encourages men to engage in caring work, for instance, by earmarking parts of paternity or parental leave especially for fathers (see later).

Family policy: key delivery mechanisms

In broad terms, we can draw a distinction between three key types of intervention in family policy: cash benefits; in-kind services; and employment rights. Many of the key issues relating to cash benefits were discussed in detail in Chapter 2, income transfers to families with children being a key element of the social security system. Where social security and family policy interact is over the question of whether and in what ways the state should play a role in supplementing the income of families with children in order to account for the increased costs a household faces when raising children. While most high-income countries provide such income top-ups, there are important variations in how they do so. First, we can draw a distinction between universal benefits paid to all families with children and targeted (also called means-tested) benefits, which are paid only to those below a certain income threshold. In addition, we can add to this picture a layer of complexity by noting that some countries use tax credits to top of the incomes of those in work (see Chapter 3). Finally, it is important to note that cash benefits for families with children vary across countries in terms of qualifying rules and rules for determining payment rates. For instance, some countries make larger payments for large families while others limit payments only to the first one or two children. Similarly, some countries pay supplements to lone-parent families while others do not (see Chapter 2).

Childcare is a good example of an in-kind service. There are some parallels here with health (see Chapter 4) insofar as the state is presented with a number of options for the provision and the financing of services. In terms of provision, in practice, most countries will have a mix of informal care (ie provided by family and friends) and formal care provided by public and/or private organisations. These options can operate somewhat independently from the financing options, which range from providing a system free at the point of use, financed by taxation, or a system that subsidises or refunds (sometimes even fully) the cost of public or private services paid for by the parent(s). Some countries use tax credits/tax reductions as a way of helping working parents meet the costs of childcare and some use vouchers that can be spent on services delivered by approved providers. As with cash benefits, governments can also choose to vary these financing options by family type and income level by, for example, targeting financial support towards lower-income families only or providing additional support for lone-parent families. This is a complex picture that reflects both the wide range of approaches in operation and also the considerable costs of providing childcare. While the state typically plays a role in moderating costs, the reality is that childcare remains a major item of household expenditure for families that require childcare, even for relatively well-off middle-class households. Figure 7.2 shows the situation for a dual-earner family with 150% of average income for a range of countries in 2012. As can be seen, while in countries such as Austria, Greece and Sweden, the typical cost was a relatively modest amount when expressed as a share of family income (under 5%) for a relatively well-off family, costs in excess of 10% were not uncommon in other countries, and in the UK, the level was in excess of one third of family income.

Figure 7.2: Out-of-pocket childcare costs[a]

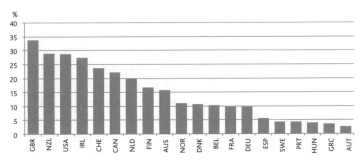

Note: [a] Childcare costs as a percentage of net family for a dual-earner family with full-time earnings of 150% of the average wage, 2012.

Source: OECD.stat.

In terms of employment rights, the main mechanisms are those providing employees with children additional rights to leave and/ or some flexibility and control over working hours in oder to accommodate caring responsibilities. A key example is maternity leave: most high-income countries give women the right to a period of employment-protected leave around childbirth – with some providing similar rights for adoption – typically accompanied by income support payments too. While some high-income countries are exceptions (at the time of writing, the US has no national scheme), most have long-established provisions but these vary in terms of the length of leave and the average payment rate. In 2013, for example, the UK provided for up to 52 weeks of leave but at an average payment rate of just 22.5% of the average wage, while in Austria, leave was just 16 weeks but with an average payment rate at 100% of the average wage (OECD, 2014c). Some analysts have suggested that countries tend to group into those providing long and thin leaves (ie lengthy periods of leave but low payment rates) or short and fat ones (high payment rates for shorter periods). Leave periods are provided in other circumstances too: most countries offer paternity leave for the fathers of newly born children, but this leave is typically of much shorter duration than is the case for maternity leave, though some countries offer a more flexible model of parental leave that allows a sharing of leave rights between two parents. Some, by contrast, allocate a portion that can only be used by fathers in order to encourage them to play an active role in childcare. This provides only a flavour of the employment rights that exist in practice; in addition to these key leaves around childbirth, some countries also allow parents paid leave when caring for a sick child and some give parents legal rights to flexible working hours in order to accommodate caring duties. Indeed, in the Netherlands, parents have a firm right to work part-time should they choose to do so and, in large part, this explains why the country has the highest percentage of part-time workers – among both men and women – within the OECD.

Family policy: key policy issues

The decision over which issues to focus on here is a challenging one, not least because competing goals for family policy mean determining what makes for a successful 'family policy' outcome is a matter for debate. Indeed, what some may see as a success (eg protecting the 'traditional' family model), others would see as a gross failure. As we hinted earlier, much contemporary family policy in high-income countries is intertwined with issues around employment and the balancing of work and family life. This policy agenda, while it has very real impacts on both family life and gender equity, also reflects economic concerns, for maximising the number of workers is often seen by governments as key to promoting economic growth. In addition, we might add that maximising the number of workers also maximises the number of taxpayers, meaning that some governments therefore see the dual-earner model as an important way of boosting the sustainability of the welfare state.

Given this, one set of outcomes for family policy might actually be labour market participation rates, particularly female and maternal employment rates as compared with male employment rates. Certainly, it has been a goal of many OECD countries to use family policies to support the move towards a dual-earner model. However, there are variations in the degree to which countries have been successful here and some countries still display large gaps between the employment rates of men and women. Figure 7.3 plots data comparing these employment gaps in 1990 and 2012. While some countries, such as Sweden and Finland, had a relatively modest gap in 1990 (around five percentage points difference between the employment rates for men and women) and maintained this low gap in 2012, countries such as France and Germany have moved from having large employment gaps in excess of 20 points to gaps of under 10 points over the same period. Those that started the 1990s with very large gaps of more than 30 points – such as Ireland, Italy, Spain and Turkey – have had mixed experiences; while Spain and Ireland have seen the gap fall to under 10 points, relatively large gaps remain in Italy and especially in Turkey. There was also little movement in the gaps in Japan and South Korea over this period, both starting and ending the period with gaps in excess of 20 points. However, despite these variations, the picture across the OECD a whole is one of shrinking employment gaps; indeed, no country in Figure 7.3 sees the gap increase and, on average, employment gaps roughly halved over this period.

Figure 7.3: Gender employment gap[a]

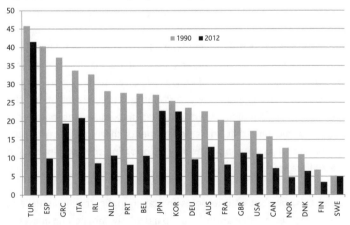

Note: [a] Percentage point difference in male and female employment rate.

Source: OECD.stat.

As we noted earlier, an equitable dual-earner model would not only support more women into the labour market, but also facilitate an expansion of caring work undertaken by men. Evidence here is harder to provide than for the expansion of work opportunities given that it concerns private activity undertaken in households. However, time-use surveys provide us with useful statistical information for some countries. The most recent data published by the OECD (for surveys completed between 2009 and 2011 [see OECD, 2014c]) shows that, across high-income countries generally, women spend significantly more time caring for household members (an average of 40 minutes per day for women, compared with 16 for men) and undertaking routine housework activities (168 minutes per day for women, compared with 74 for men). Meanwhile, men spend, on average, more time than women watching/listening to the TV/radio (123 minutes for men, compared to 74 for women) and in sporting activity (26 minutes for men, compared with 18 for women). It seems, therefore, that we have some way to go before achieving true gender equity.

Birth-related leaves such as maternity and paternity leave have, in part, been extended in some countries because of concerns around declining fertility rates in recent decades. Across high-income countries, there was a steady decline in the average number of children born per woman from the late-1960s/early-1970s onwards. For example, from 1970 to 1995, the number of children per woman (the total fertility rate) fell from: 2.48 to 1.71 in France; 2.43 to 1.19 in Italy; 4.53 to 1.63 in South Korea; 2.90 to 1.17 in Spain; 2.48 to 1.98 in the US; and 2.43 to 1.70 in the UK. Broadly speaking, a fertility rate below the replacement level of 2.1 will result in a falling population without immigration, adding to the 'demographic time bomb' issues for financing welfare covered in Chapter 2. In each of the examples we give here, the drop is particularly significant because the countries move from a fertility rate *above* 2.1 to a level *below* this. In most of these countries, in part, due to expanding family policies, fertility rates have increased between 1995 and 2012, albeit remaining below the replacement level of 2.1. Whether low fertility rates are a concern for social policy or private choices that do not concern the state is a moot point. However, there is some evidence from surveys that those living in high-income countries are, on average, having fewer children than they would see as ideal; if this is so, then it might be argued that family policy needs to go further in allowing people to balance work and family life.

Some argue that family policies can ultimately be judged on the basis of whether they improve the well-being of children and young people. 'Well-being' is a very broad concept and, when used in this context, might relate to a wide range of outcomes relevant to the lives of children and young people. In recent years, the United Nations Children's Fund (UNICEF) has produced several reports that aim to measure the level of child well-being in rich countries (eg UNICEF, 2007, 2013). In these studies, UNICEF have combined information on many topics, including income poverty, immunisation rates, educational attainment, healthy eating, bullying/fighting at school, risky behaviours such as taking drugs and the quality of living environments. In its 2013 study, which covered 29 countries, the highest levels of child well-being were found in the Netherlands and the Nordic countries, while the US, Lithuania, Latvia and Romania fared worst. Those countries with the highest levels of child well-being are, for the most part, those with the most extensive family policies.

As we have stressed, we can only touch the surface of some very complex and important debates in this short review of family policy. As the discussion should make clear, there are some complex policy challenges here that raise fundamental questions about where public and private concerns start and end. Moreover, family policy is central in shaping the transition to, and nature of, the post-industrial economy, for this new economy is typically very different from the traditional industrial economy not only in terms of the types of jobs people do (ie service sector jobs predominate), but also in terms of who does them (ie we observe a move away from a male-breadwinner model as female participation rates increase). How far family policy facilitates this move by removing barriers to employment is key, but so, too, is how social policy reshapes traditional gender roles in the family (see Box 7.1). This issue is also key in the second policy area that we offer a mini-tour of: social care.

Social care

Social care: key policy goals

As with family policy, the range of policies that might fall under the heading of social care is contested. Indeed, some analysts, particularly outside the UK, would regard childcare as one of the key policy areas within social care. Some theorists have suggested that we should simply talk of 'care' in generic terms rather than of social care as the concept of care cuts right across the standard pillars of the welfare state and shows it in a different light, particularly in terms of how social policy shapes gender relations in society by capturing both state-provided ('social') care and care provided through the market and by the family. There is much to be said for this approach, and while we focus on the basics here, we encourage readers to go further in exploring such arguments (see the reading guide at end of chapter for suggestions in this regard).

As we have examined childcare already, we exclude this here, focusing on a definition of social care that includes policies such as: care for older people; services to support disabled people; care for vulnerable adults, such as people with mental health problems; protective services for children and young people deemed at risk of significant harm; and care for children and young people beyond the more general services and benefits covered by the family policies outlined earlier. This perhaps captures the notion of social care as commonly used in the UK, but given that there is dispute over the policies that fall under this heading internationally, providing figures for spending across countries is problematic and the OECD, for example, do not provide robust and comparable data relating directly to this definition. However, we can provide data covering some aspects relating to social care services and do so in Figure 7.4.

As can be seen, there are clear variations between countries; while the Scandinavian countries, in particular, devote significant proportions of GDP to this area – 5% in Sweden and almost 4% in Denmark, for example – in countries such as Canada, New Zealand and the US,

Figure 7.4: Social care spending[a]

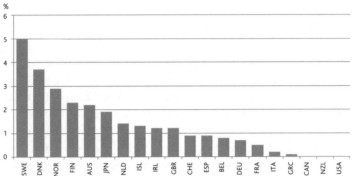

Note: [a] Public spending on old-age and incapacity-related in-kind benefits plus family home help/accommodation as a percentage of gross domestic product (GDP), 2011.

Source: OECD.stat.

the figure is very close to zero. Jensen (2008) suggests that these differences in spending on care can be usefully related to differences in social security spending, which reveals three distinct patterns of activity that point to differing goals for social care policy across countries. First, we have Scandinavian countries, where spending on both cash benefits and social care is high. This, Jensen suggests, is linked to an ideological commitment to gender equity in which the state plays a comparatively strong role in social care in order to move society away from the traditional family model. Second, we have countries such as Canada and the US, where spending on both cash benefits and social care are low. Jensen argues that in these countries, social policy has been driven by a preference to keep state involvement in welfare low, the implications for individual households therefore partly depending on the income that they can generate through the market in order to buy private care services to replace the care provided by the family and to supplement the minimal care provided by the state. Finally, there are countries such as France, Germany and Italy, where spending on cash benefits is relatively high but spending on social care is quite low. Jensen argues that these countries have not had an ideological preference against state intervention (far from it given the high levels of social security spending), but that social care spending has been suppressed by an ideological bias towards traditional family models. In these societies, we might expect families to play a larger role in providing care, with relatively strong traditional gender norms meaning that women provide most of this care in practice.

Social care: key delivery mechanisms

As with our discussion of family policy, the range of policy interventions deployed under the heading of 'social care' is hugely diverse, so we simplify matters here by drawing out examples in a small number of key areas. Again, our guide to further reading points to resources that go further than is possible here.

In most high-income countries, the biggest area of social care in terms of expenditure is care for older people. We perhaps should say at the outset that the majority of older people do not require care and, on the contrary, many older people, in fact, act as carers – for example, by looking after other family members. In principle, the delivery mechanisms here could be deemed largely the same as those discussed earlier for the care of children, that is, cash benefits, in-kind services and employment rights for carers. However, there are, of course, important differences given that these policies are not aimed at children. In particular, while family members often provide care to their older relatives, very few countries provide such carers with rights to time off from work to anywhere near the extent that they do for carers of children and, in terms of cash benefits, few systems provide specific additional payments beyond the standard pension system, though some do provide cash transfers to carers in some circumstances, albeit usually rather modest payments.

Consequently, care for older people mainly comprises in-kind care services that, broadly speaking, can take two key forms: residential care (sometimes called institutional care) or home-based care (sometimes called community care). These two types of formal care (ie provided by organisations) are supplements to informal care (ie provided by family and/or friends). However, the balance between these different elements varies hugely across countries, in line with the variations in spending noted earlier. So, for example: Sweden and the Netherlands have relatively extensive residential and home-based care services; Canada places a stronger emphasis on residential care services than home-based care, but in Japan, the opposite is true; and some countries, such as Greece and Portugal, rely heavily on informal care, the state providing only minimal formal care (Bettio and Plantenga, 2004; Colombo et al, 2011). In practice, care usually comprises a mixture of formal and informal care. Likewise, it should be noted that formal care services can be provided by the state or by the market and, again, a mix of the two is not uncommon, and even where services are funded through taxation, they are often delivered by private organisations. In other words, care for older people often involves a complex mixed economy of provision.

This is reflected in mechanisms for financing longer-term care for older people, which is a particularly acute policy challenge in many high-income countries because ageing populations and rising life expectancy mean that costs are rising and expected to grow still further in many countries over coming decades. The mechanisms here are similar to those for healthcare discussed in Chapter 4. Around one third of OECD countries have a universal tax-funded scheme, some funded through general taxation (the case in most Nordic countries), others through a specific social insurance scheme (eg this is the case in Germany and the Netherlands). Some countries provide cash payments or vouchers that can be used in support of care (eg Austria, Australia), while some (the US and UK, excluding Scotland) have targeted safety net systems where the costs of care are supported on a means-tested basis (Colombo et al, 2011). Some countries also encourage citizens to take out private long-term care insurance, though this is not widespread in any country. We should also add that cost sharing – where both the government and service user bear some of the cost – is commonplace, with rules about the contribution expected from individuals varying. As with childcare, the out-of-pocket payments made in some countries represent a very large share of disposable income for the households concerned and often draw heavily on assets, such as savings or housing equity.

Services that supplement or replace the informal care that might be provided to support friends or family perhaps offer the most commonly understood dimension of social care. However, perhaps less commonly invoked by the notion of 'social care', but central to the sector, are protective services designed to safeguard children deemed at risk of abuse or neglect. These services, typically the responsibility of social work professionals but also likely to involve those from other sectors, including criminal justice, education and health at times, mix aspects of care and control insofar as they aim not just to intervene in order to protect children, but also to prevent adults (and sometimes children and young people) behaving in particular ways that might harm the welfare of a child or young person. In some cases, this might even involve them being removed from their family in order to safeguard their welfare. This highlights in one of the most extreme ways that the boundaries between the roles of the state and the family in promoting welfare are extremely fuzzy and that the appropriate boundaries between public and private concerns can often be contingent on the circumstances of individual households. Similarly, policy interventions in such areas often involve a mix of measures designed to support parents and to police or punish them. While, in some cases, the decisions here will be straightforward, in many cases, this is not so; determining if neglect or emotional abuse are issues, for instance, will often be very challenging and involve those working with the individual families concerned making complex decisions on the basis of their professional knowledge. Indeed, an international review of this area noted that even across culturally similar countries such as Australia, the UK and the US, there was a great deal of ambiguity concerning the definition of neglect and emotional abuse (Munro and Manful, 2010).

Social care: key policy issues

The breadth of this area of policy means that we can only pick out a small number of big-picture issues here. Box 7.1 explores how social care and family policies shape state, market and family relations in societies.

With regard to more discrete issues, we noted earlier that the rising costs of providing long-term care are a concern in many countries, particularly as many high-income countries expect to see rapidly increasing shares of their population to be aged over 80 years, this group comprising the majority of recipients of care. Alongside this ageing of societies, other social policy changes such as later retirement ages, declining fertility rates and increased labour market participation are shrinking the availability of informal carers. Consequently, a key challenge is not merely financing long-term care, but also securing an adequate number of carers in the workforce. Across the OECD, the number of workers required in this sector is expected to double by 2050 (Colombo et al, 2011). For some countries, particularly those where pay is low in much of the sector perhaps, this presents a real challenge.

One of the challenges that we have faced in assembling this mini-tour of the social care sector is that the diverse range of policy areas it covers means that there are overlaps with many other policy sectors. This is a challenge in real-world policy also, with social care policies and social care services often interacting uneasily with policies and services in healthcare, education, social security, housing and criminal justice. Some suggest that social care might be seen as the glue that binds these different services together, working with individuals with often complex needs and requiring support from a range of different organisations often at a moment when their lives are in the midst of a major transition. Some also describe this as a forgotten or underappreciated sector that often loses out to more prominent and powerful sectors such as health in the battle for resources. A seemingly perennial debate around social care, therefore, is how social care services can be integrated more effectively with healthcare, education, criminal justice and so on.

Finally, we should note that while the word 'care' invokes well-meaning protective notions, the other side of the coin is that social care policies can serve to increase control over people's lives and/or reduce their autonomy and independence. We have noted some examples earlier but might usefully add some more in order to underline these key issues. Issues around autonomy and independence have been particularly significant in disability policy. Indeed, the concept of independent living has been central to debates in recent decades, with most countries moving away from residential services in favour of more flexible delivery mechanisms that give disabled people autonomy to devise packages of services that support community living. This might include measures such as giving disabled people budgets that they control in order to purchase the support that they find most helpful. While this might sound like an eminently sensible approach, balancing independence and care in practice can be complex. Indeed, moves in this direction have been seen by some as providing governments with cover for reducing their responsibilities in this sector, the language of flexibility and individual care packages masking the fragmentation of public services and patchy service coverage.

Box 7.1 Family–state–market interactions

In Chapter 1, we introduced Esping-Andersen's (1990) classic analysis of welfare systems across high-income countries, in which he argued that three different types of welfare system could be identified based on varying social rights, social stratification and the role played by the state, market and family in the delivery of welfare. However, critics suggested that his work provided a class-based analysis that overlooked important gender inequalities in society, which was exacerbated by a relatively narrow exploration of the role of the family (rather than the state or market) in providing welfare.

Esping-Andersen (1999) acknowledged these criticisms in a subsequent work, developing the concept of defamilialisation to capture the ways in which social policies might alter traditional caring roles by expanding the role of the state (and so diminishing the dependence on the family) in the provision of care. By examining data on a range of care-related services, Esping-Andersen argued that defamilialisation could add much to our understanding of welfare systems, particularly their role in shaping gender roles, though it did not alter his classification of welfare states insofar as he found strong overlaps between analyses rooted in class and gender perspectives. Specifically, he said we could observe:

- Social democratic countries with strong social security systems and a high degree of defamilialisation. High levels of income equity and high levels of gender equity went hand in hand here, with many women finding work in care-related public services.
- Liberal countries with weak social security systems and a low degree of defamilialisation, but with labour markets showing relatively high levels of female participation. As such, much depended on the income position of households in relatively unequal societies: those with sufficient money were well-placed to defamilialise by purchasing care-related services from private markets, with those without much less so.
- Conservative/corporatist countries with strong social security systems but a low degree of defamilialisation. These countries tended to display relatively low levels of income inequality across social classes, but important gender differences remained, particularly in terms of employment, where a male-breadwinner model was the norm and where women often had to choose between a working career and family life.

There have been some important changes since his analysis was completed – for example, key conservative/corporatist countries such as Germany have seen female labour market participation rise – but many of the core observations remain pertinent. In particular, the social democratic countries (mainly the Nordic states) remain the exemplars of gender equity (albeit with inequities remaining), while in the liberal countries, there are pressures on many women as their labour market participation rates are high but public care services remain patchy and men have yet to take a more equal role in caring tasks. As noted, many of the conservative/corporatist states have started to shift towards a dual-earner model too, though some – such as Italy – remain a good distance from this approach and policy frameworks continue to offer low levels of defamilialisation in most instances.

Criminal justice

Criminal justice: key policy goals

The final policy area we consider in this chapter is criminal justice. Although not traditionally seen as forming a central pillar of the welfare state, it nonetheless plays a key role in promoting well-being by protecting personal safety (note, for instance, the overlaps here with elements of child well-being discussed earlier). At the same time, ensuring the just operation of the legal system is an essential part of creating a fair society; indeed, an ill-functioning criminal justice system is a fundamental threat to liberty. However, aside from these abstract observations, it is generally agreed that criminal justice is an area of policy that has risen up the political agenda in many countries over recent decades. Criminal justice is now firmly established as one of the major political issues and it is not uncommon for political parties to seek to outbid their opponents during election campaigns on the question of who will be 'toughest' on crime. While much of the administration of criminal justice is in the hands of supposedly impartial instruments of the law, such as the police and law courts, the fact that criminal justice has become the focus of election battles underlines that, in reality, it is a highly politicised field. Debates concerning what constitutes crime, the ways in which crimes should be punished and, indeed, the ultimate societal goals of the criminal justice system are as much political questions as they are technical or legal ones.

In comparing criminal justice systems across countries, it is more difficult to rely on comparisons of spending levels as we have done for other policy areas. However, in exploring key policy goals, we can draw a broad distinction between systems rooted in punitive penalism and those rooted in penal welfarism. In the former, the emphasis is on the punishment of offenders, those breaking laws often serving relatively lengthy sentences and perhaps the key goal of policy being to use heavy punishment as a deterrent to crime. In the latter, there is more emphasis placed on rehabilitation, where (with the exception of some of the most serious crimes) policy aims to reform behaviours and reintegrate those who break laws. There are subtle but important models of thinking underpinning these two systems. Punitive penalism has a somewhat *individualistic and rational actor view* of the world, where crime is presumed to be perpetrated by individuals acting in a calculated way and so strong punishments are administered on the basis that they should act to deter people from breaking the law. Penal welfarism has a *more structural perspective*, where crime is also assumed to have complex social roots. Indeed, part of the penal welfarism model typically involves addressing socioeconomic disadvantage more seriously than is the case in countries pursuing punitive penalism.

Criminal justice: key delivery mechanisms

We should stress that, in practice, all countries have an often uneasy mixture of overlapping policies rooted in elements of both punitive penalism and penal welfarism, but a consideration of variations in the deployment of some of the key policy delivery mechanisms makes clear that the variations between countries in the mix of these approaches is important. For example, use of what might be seen as the most basic policy instrument in criminal justice – prison – varies starkly across the rich countries. Figure 7.5 displays the incarceration rate – measured as the number of prisoners per 100,000 of the population – for 30 countries in 2012. The US stands out as an exceptional case, with an incarceration rate of 701.8 per 100,000 of the population, one of the highest rates in the world and certainly very unusual among high-income democracies. A comparison of this with the incarceration rates of countries at the other end of the chart makes clear how extreme the US case is: in Japan, the rate is just 52.7, and in Finland, it is 61.1, but even countries with relatively high rates are a long way from the levels of imprisonment found in the US. The UK (here, data is for England and Wales), for example, has a rate of 150.1, less than a quarter of that for the US. Indeed, the US's incarceration rate is

Figure 7.5: Incarceration rate[a]

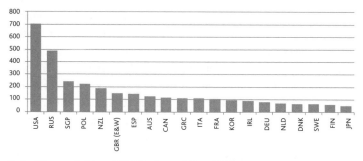

Note: [a] Persons held per 100,000 of population, 2012 or nearest year.

Source: UNODC.org

comfortably more than double that of even the third-highest country in our chart, Singapore, which has a rate of 244.7. While there will, of course, be variations in the level of crime across countries, such stark variations in the incarceration rate cannot be explained by this and instead reflect differences in sentencing practice. Put simply, the US is more likely to lock someone up for breaking the law and to lock them up for longer too.

Comparing crime rates across countries only offers a partial picture of criminal justice policy because of variations in the ways in which crime is recorded and, indeed, what counts as a crime in each country. However, specially designed international crime and victim surveys allow us to make some useful comparisons, albeit with somewhat dated statistics. We present some data from the United Nations Interregional Crime and Justice Research Institute's (UNICRI, 2000) International Crime Victims Survey in Table 7.1. Interestingly, while the data does show variation in victimisation rates across countries, it is not so nearly dramatic as the variation in incarceration rates, underlining the fact that the link between the two is mediated by policy choices around the degree of penalism. Indeed, in some areas of crime, the US showed a lower victimisation rate than average for the sample of countries included in the survey (eg car theft, robbery and sexual incidents).

The weak link between victimisation rates and imprisonment rates underlines the fact that criminal justice, far from being a merely technical-legal issue, is deeply political, with debates around what is a crime and how transgressions should be handled very normative issues. This can be further illustrated by simply examining the varying ways in which different countries respond to particular issues. A straightforward example here is provided by policy around cannabis, which is the most used illicit drug globally (UNODC, 2011). In the UK, cannabis is classified as a 'Class B' drug, deemed less severe than

Table 7.1: Victimisation[a]

	Car theft	Burglary	Robbery	Sexual incidents	Assaults and threats
Australia	2.0	4.8	1.5	7.5	11.2
Belgium	0.9	2.4	1.4	2.1	4.6
Canada	1.4	2.9	1.2	3.8	8.5
Denmark	1.2	3.3	0.8	4.6	4.7
England and Wales	2.4	3.4	2.0	6.1	12.4
France	2.0	1.0	1.8	1.3	6.0
Japan	0.1	1.7	0.1	3.1	0.6
Poland	1.1	2.5	2.5	0.5	5.4
Sweden	1.4	2.3	1.5	6.0	6.5
United States	0.6	3.3	0.6	2.8	6.5
Average across all 17 countries in survey	1.0	2.3	1.2	3.6	5.9

Note: [a] Number of offences per 100 inhabitants, 1999.

Source: UNICRI (2000).

drugs such as heroin but nonetheless regarded as a substance that it is illegal to both supply and possess, with prison terms of up to 14 years for supply and up to five years for possession of cannabis existing under current laws. Although classified as a controlled substance in key international conventions, some countries have adopted rather different policy frameworks to the UK. Most famously, perhaps, the Netherlands has allowed the possession and sale of small amounts of cannabis under certain conditions since the 1970s, with around 1,000 'coffee shops' selling the drug at the discretion of local authorities. Some countries, notably Portugal, have decriminalised the possession and personal use of cannabis. That said, we should also note that how policies around the control of cannabis operate on the ground will, to a good degree, depend on the discretion of law enforcement agencies; indeed, a recent review of policy in this area suggested that in most high-income countries, there is very little risk of someone being criminally penalised for cannabis use even when laws carry notionally tough penalties (UNODC, 2011). A fuller exploration of policy mechanisms in this area might note not just the legal penalties (or lack thereof) for the possession of cannabis, but also the frameworks in place to prevent cannabis use and to treat those who have become dependent on it. Here, there may be significant overlaps with other areas of policy, particularly health, and access to relevant services (eg drug treatment programmes) will, to a large extent, be shaped by policy decisions made by those working outside the criminal justice sector.

Criminal justice: key policy issues

There is much debate over the question of whether a more punitive approach is successful in bringing down levels of crime, particularly around the US experience, but the analytic issues are complex. The US's extreme punitiveness does not leave it with the lowest levels of crime in the OECD, far from it, as demonstrated in . However, because there are many factors that might influence underlying levels of crime beyond the punitiveness of criminal justice policy – including economic, social and technological factors – we should not expect a clear link between incarceration rates and crime rates across countries. What we can say with a higher degree of confidence when looking across high-income countries, however, is that, broadly speaking, they break down into two categories: those with extensive welfare systems, less punitive criminal justice systems, lower levels of inequality and lower levels of imprisonment; and those with more minimal welfare systems, more punitive criminal justice systems, higher levels of inequality and higher levels of imprisonment. This, of course, is a simplification, but one that captures broad differences in how behaviours deemed transgressive might be handled; indeed, Greenberg (2001: 81) has suggested that 'locking people up or giving them money might be considered alternative ways of handling marginal poor populations – repressive in one case, generous in the other'.

However, while we can observe important differences between countries, many theorists suggest there has been a tendency towards increased punitiveness in most high-income countries in recent decades, as part of an increased emphasis on individual behaviours – rather than social factors – being seen as the key cause of crime. Some theorists have connected this with a trend of growing social control of the poorest in society more generally, which also includes increased conditionality in social security and employment services, with harsh sanctions for those failing to display stipulated behaviours (see Chapter 2). Indeed, Wacquant (2009) argues that governments have increased the social control of the poorest in order to appear tough for political reasons, masking their inability or unwillingness to protect citizens from economic risks by shouting loudly about the need to protect people from 'deviant' groups in society. To this end, he argues, we should talk of 'prisonfare' alongside the notion of 'workfare' (see Chapter 3), on the basis that the two are interconnected social policy reforms. While Wacquant's argument states the case more boldly than most would – there is much debate over how far his thesis truly matches the evidence – there is nonetheless plenty of evidence to support claims that there has been increased social control of the poorest in many countries.

We noted earlier that comparing national crime rates across countries only offers a partial picture of the operation of criminal justice.

Another reason that this is so is because these headline figures tell us nothing about *who* is being imprisoned and why. For England and Wales, a brief examination of the relevant statistical data underlines that those who have been disadvantaged socially and economically make up a disproportionate share of prisoners: for instance, almost 50% of prisoners have no qualifications (compared with 15% of people nationally), around 50% of young offenders were excluded from school and around 15% of newly sentenced offenders were homeless before entering custody (Prison Reform Trust, 2013). In many countries, it is also the case that inequalities associated with economic disadvantage intersect with other social divisions and this adds another important dimension to analyses of how criminal justice policy operates in practice. One of the starkest examples here is found in the US. We highlighted the exceptionally punitive nature of its system when discussing the data in Figure 7.5, but it is vital to understanding criminal justice in the US to be aware of the fact that its imprisonment varies hugely by ethnicity: in 2010, the incarceration rate for black people was around 6.5 times higher than that for white people (Bureau of Justice Statistics, 2011). Typically, probing beneath the national figures reveals uneven patterns in terms of which groups are most/least likely to be imprisoned, reflecting differences in the power of different groups and, ultimately, the social construction of crime. For instance, extremely wealthy individuals evading tax are rarely pursued as vigorously or treated as harshly for their transgressions as lower-income people who have fraudulently claimed social security benefits, even though the losses to the state are usually much greater from the former than the latter. It is these kinds of issues that Wacquant highlights when arguing that criminal justice policy has been used to control the poor as an alternative to expanding other areas of social policy in order to support the poor.

The debate over whether punitive or welfare-based approaches should be emphasised has a heightened significance in policy frameworks around young people. Children and young people have often been protected from the full weight of the law on the basis that childhood is a developmental stage of life; this is recognised in the United Nations Convention on the Rights of the Child, which places emphasis on the need to protect children and, in respect to the justice system, provide treatment that is distinct from the treatment of adults. However, even across neighbouring European countries, there are major variations in the age at which criminal responsibility begins (ie the age from which someone can be prosecuted for a crime), reflecting differing views on how far young people should be protected from the law: in Belgium, it is 16 years of age; in Norway, it is 15; in Italy, it is 14; in France, it is 13; in Ireland, it is 12; and in England and Wales, it is just 10 years of age (Hazel, 2008). There are also important differences across countries in the mechanisms used to hear the evidence of potentially transgressive behaviour and in how instances deemed transgressive are resolved. While inquisitorial court-type processes similar to those used for adults are common, some countries place an emphasis on restorative justice as an alternative to this: New Zealand, for example, pioneered family group conferences some time ago as an alternative to prosecution, where the young person, their family and the victim are involved in a process of mediated decision-making designed to reaching a group consensus on a 'just' resolution. While many view such restorative approaches positively, Muncie and Goldson (2006: 199) argue that, just as has occurred for adults, recent decades have seen many governments increasingly favour punitive approaches over welfare approaches as the 'emphasis has become one of fighting juvenile crime rather than securing juvenile justice'.

Once again, we have only been able to touch on a very small number of key issues in our review here and so we remind readers for a final time to consult the additional reading guide if they wish to explore issues further. However, even in this brief review of key issues, we have hopefully underlined how criminal justice policy necessarily interacts with, rather than operating in isolation from, the welfare state.

KEY READING GUIDE

Many of the extended introductory Social Policy texts have chapters covering the policy sectors examined here. Pahl's (2012) chapter on 'The family and welfare' in Baldock et al's (2012) *Social policy* and the chapter by Millar and Haux (2012) on 'Family policy' in Alcock et al's (2012) *The student's companion to social policy* are particularly useful. For social care, Hill and Irving (2009) provide good reviews of services in chapters 8 and 9 of their book; several chapters in Alcock et al's (2012) *The student's companion to social policy* are relevant, particularly Glasby's (2012) chapter 'Social care'. For criminal justice, Eadie and Morley (2012) provide a useful chapter in Baldock et al's (2012) *Social policy* and Newburn (2012a) provides a good introduction in Alcock et al's (2012) *The student's companion to social policy*.

There are numerous textbooks that offer more detailed accounts of each area – and even areas within each area – covered within this chapter. For criminal justice, Newburn's (2012b) *Criminology* offers a comprehensive introduction and Wincup's (2013) *Understanding crime and social policy* helps link these two subject areas together. Adams's (2010) *The short guide to social work* provides an accessible overview of many of the areas we touch on in our review of social care. Disability studies is a social science subject in its own right and there are many textbooks in this area: *Understanding disability policy* by Roulstone and Prideaux (2012) is a particularly useful introduction to this area for students of Social Policy, while Priestley's (2012) chapter on 'Disability' in Alcock et al's (2012) *The student's companion to social policy* offers an excellent short overview. An excellent overview of many of the issues covered in our discussion of family policy can be found in Lewis's (2009) *Work–family balance, gender and policy.*

The OECD provides a lot of easily accessible information on family policy and family life on its website, as well as some information about care services (see: www.oecd.org/; for specialised information on family policy, see also: www.oecd.org/els/family/). EUROSTAT provides detailed cross-national crime statistics for Europe (see: http://ec.europa.eu/eurostat/statistics-explained/index.php/Crime_statistics), while UNICRI provide data and publications with a more global reach (see: www.unicri.it/).

8

conclusion

Introduction

In our short tour of some of the key sights of social policy, we have covered a lot of ground: the five key areas of welfare plus the new pillars of family, social care and criminal justice policy; examples and evidence from more than 60 different countries; some key conceptual arguments; numerous policy issues; and an array of often competing policy mechanisms. Yet, we must emphasise that this is only a *short* guide: as we said at the start of the book, we have constrained ourselves to a tour of the major 'boulevards' of social policy. There is still, of course, much more to be seen and much more to be said.

So far, we have largely written about the pillars as though they are separate, discreet entities not connected to each other. As we have suggested at times, in reality, this is not the case, and as a consequence, we have to acknowledge some doubt about discussing them as we have done in separate chapters. Our decision to offer a separate treatment of each pillar simply arises from the fact that this is a short introductory text and we have to begin somewhere. Or, in other words, we need to simplify the often beguiling complexity of the real world in order to offer a less complex analysis of it. However, as we draw the book to a close, it is very important to remind readers that:

- there are important interrelationships between the major pillars of welfare we have discussed;
- the pillars of welfare have a broad significance that extends beyond the issues we have covered here;

- there are other ways of thinking about social policies than our emphasis on pillars and policy mechanisms; and
- we have focused our attention on the 'what' questions of social policy (ie what the pillars look like), but there are important 'why' questions that need to be addressed too (ie why countries tackle common social problems in different ways).

In this chapter, we want to briefly reflect on these points and so will:

- offer some thoughts on how the pillars we have already toured relate to each other;
- highlight the broader dimensions that our key pillars operate within; and
- underline the crucial role that broader theoretical perspectives must play in providing an understanding of the 'why' questions in social policy analysis.

The five 'giants' of welfare and beyond

Taking our cue from Beveridge (1942), we initially focused our attention in this short guide on the five 'giants' of welfare: social security, employment, education, health and housing. Given that we analysed these pillars independently, it is worth us spending a little time reflecting on how they relate to one another. Much social policy research has uncovered significant differences in the nature of welfare states across countries. Despite the fact that they deal with common risks and contingencies, social policies addressing, say, healthcare needs do not always share the same goals in different countries, with some offering universally available public healthcare and others favouring private provision. Some analysts have suggested that we can see different 'welfare regimes' across the world, with very different types of welfare system in place in different countries around the world (Esping-Andersen, 1990).

Sometimes, we take for granted how things work in our own society or own lives and can fall into the trap of thinking that much of what we see is the norm. Therefore, the comparison of our own situation with those in other places is a very valuable tool for helping us learn about ourselves. This is true for our personal life as well as for the analysis of social policies. For instance, we can only tell whether we are tall or short if we know how we compare to others around us. Equally, we can only know whether a certain country has generous or lean social policies if we compare them to those in other societies. This is the primary reason behind our decision to use a comparative and global approach in this short guide. This is also the reason why – in our mind – comparative and global social policy research has produced much of the most interesting and thought-provoking work in Social Policy in recent years.

We should not underestimate the importance of differences between nations' social policies. It is in the detail of social policy mechanisms that we find the fundamental differences of alternative welfare state models and, indeed, fundamental differences in the nature of capitalism within nations. For instance, whether the social security system favours a high degree of income redistribution or simply provides a safety net for a relatively small, targeted group of people tells us a great deal about a nation's (or, perhaps, more accurately, its government's) attitudes towards the allocation of rewards in society and, in turn, its views on the legitimacy of monetary inequalities generated by the free market. We should not forget either that these big macro-level differences in the nature of capitalisms are also played out at the micro-level: differences in social policy mechanisms fundamentally shape people's everyday lives. For example, whether a state takes responsibility for providing comprehensive childcare facilities or whether it allows parents to undertake flexible working hours can influence the chosen career paths of parents and, indeed, influence adults' decisions over whether to have children. For children, different curricula may, for instance, determine the ability to speak different foreign languages, and may have an influence on career opportunities in later life. We have discussed many more such examples throughout this book. While we have focused our attention on providing statistical evidence of national differences, it is important to understand that different social policies do not simply alter statistics, but have a crucial impact on the everyday-life realities of millions of individuals.

In other words, policy goals and delivery mechanisms are very closely related to each other. A nation that aims to redistribute incomes to a large extent can hardly rely solely on targeted, means-tested benefits. Equally, the aim of status maintenance in conservative countries cannot be achieved by providing very generous universal benefits across the board. While the phrase 'policy mechanisms' may give the impression that social policy is concerned with technical choices between different instruments, we should never lose sight of the fact that these competing mechanisms often embody different values and principles.

We discussed numerous policy issues in our exploration of the pillars. These policy issues also relate – at least to some extent – to the existing delivery mechanisms in different countries. While there is a long-running debate about whether, in practice, one model of welfare is better than another, it is relatively rare to see nations switch between mechanisms in a radical way. Instead, much policy making in each country involves patching up the weaknesses found within already-chosen mechanisms rather than the implementation of far-reaching alternatives. In other words, because nations have quite different combinations of social policy mechanisms, the nature of policy debate in each country can often be quite different too, even when they are responding to common longer-term pressures for change caused by global economic competition and the ageing of the population, or to sudden improbable shocks such as the recent global financial and economic crises (Farnsworth and Irving, 2011). This is an important point, for it suggests that there is rarely one 'right' policy choice that can be pointed to as the best solution for a given problem (Rose, 2005); instead, different countries often require different solutions to similar problems.

Significantly, the policy mechanisms deployed in one pillar of welfare can shape the policy issues faced in another. So, whether a nation actually faces a pensions funding crisis is not only a consequence of the financing mechanism and generosity of pensions, but also – at least partly – caused by increasing life expectancy and persistent low levels of fertility, decisions that may be influenced by health, employment and broader social security policies. The issue of skills shortages is not only caused by processes of deindustrialisation and the growth of the service sector of the labour market, but can be facilitated or aggravated by specific focal points in education and migration policies. These examples also help to show that single pillars never work in a vacuum. In reality, every social policy pillar is interacting with each other. So, for example, programmes designed to alleviate poverty in the long run cannot be based solely on income protection schemes: as we have shown, the employment, health, education and housing pillars also have an important role to play. Improvements in the education sector will not alone reach the aim of increasing human development across all segments of society, but will rely on accompanying efforts to diminish education gaps and enhance social mobility. Equally, the aim of providing an adequate number of dwellings is never simply about housing per se – decisions in this pillar are likely to radiate across all other sectors of policy making as well.

The interconnectedness of many of the key policy dilemmas is one of the reasons why policy delivery is such a complicated aspect of government. It is rarely the case that the state can single-handedly or even in partnership with private market agencies deliver a finished policy solution. One of the major lessons of policy making is that policy can be significantly *remade* during its implementation – by civil servants, by front-line workers and, indeed, by service users themselves. The policy-making process literature explores issues surrounding the complexity of making policy decisions in the real world in great depth and we should stress here how difficult it is in practice to grapple with very complex and interrelated policy dilemmas (see Hudson and Lowe, 2009). Rarely is there an obvious solution to the key policy issues that we have explored here, not least because the interconnectedness of policy pillars in practice makes it difficult to predict how a change in one part of one pillar will impact on the functioning of another part of the same pillar or, indeed, other pillars.

However, what is sometimes overlooked is that *within countries*, the respective social security, employment, education, health and housing pillars themselves can function completely differently. While it would make for a very straightforward analysis if some countries had extensive social policies in each pillar of welfare and others had minimal social policies in each pillar, the real world shows much more diversity. Indeed, just as governments in different countries make choices about which mechanisms to deploy in each sector, many also make choices over which pillar to bias their investment towards. So, for instance, the US has comparatively high levels of public education spending but low levels of support for the unemployed.

What all this suggests is that social policies rarely have a very narrow and confined impact, nor do they have simple foundations or origins. In fact, it is the very wide-ranging significance and complexity of social policies in the real world that has led to the expanding scope of concern of Social Policy as an academic subject and, likewise, an increasing interest in social policy among scholars and students of other academic subjects. Importantly, this requires us to engage with ideas and debates found in a whole series of related social science subject areas.

The inclusion of discussion on the new pillars of welfare, that is, family, social care and criminal justice (see Chapter 7), reflects the fact that the subjects of Sociology and Social Policy have always been very closely related. Indeed, in many universities, the two subjects are co-located in a single school or department and joint study of the two is commonplace. In part, this is because the social issues and social problems that concern sociologists are fundamentally shaped by social policies and, likewise, the social problems and issues that social policies seek to address are connected to the basic structures of our societies and are fundamentally shaped by powerful social forces. There has also long been a strong overlap between the subject matter studied in Social Work and Social Policy (see Adams, 2002, 2010), and Criminology and Social Policy (see Knepper, 2007; Wincup, 2013).

Less obvious, but increasingly important, links are being made between Social Policy and Geography (see Valentine, 2001) and, similarly, Social

Policy and Environmental Science (see Huby, 1998; Snell and Haq, 2014). Social policies always have a spatial element in that they are targeted towards a particular country or region. However, more than this, the issues that they address often have particularly significant spatial dimensions: unemployment might be higher in particular regions of a country or poverty more heavily concentrated in particular parts of a city, for instance. Likewise, debates about sustainable development within environmental science have led to a greater understanding of the interrelationship between social and environmental issues. In particular, there is an increasing recognition that people at higher risk of social exclusion are also often those most likely to live in the most polluted or dangerous areas. Globally, it is also largely true that the poorest nations are those most likely to bear the greatest impact of global warming.

Last, but not certainly not least, although often seen as polar opposites in the social sciences – one being concerned with markets, the other with the state – there are, in fact, important links to be made between the subjects of Economics and Social Policy, and, again, it is not uncommon for the two to be studied together. Certainly, the topics examined by each often heavily overlap: the concern with (un) employment, for example, is central to both, although the manner in which the topic is explored – and the nature of the questions addressed – differ. While, for a long time, a major debate concerned whether extensive social policies might be economically damaging (see Pfaller et al, 1991), there is an increasing recognition that, conversely, social policies themselves might be important tools for economic growth, not least because a well-educated and well-trained workforce is likely to be a more economically competitive one (European Commission, 2010; see also: http://ec.europa.eu/europe2020). Political scientists have also had a long-running interest in social policies, not least questions surrounding how social policies are created (see Hudson and Lowe, 2009) and why nations veer towards particular policy solutions (more on which later).

From what to why

Social policy, then, has a wide relevance that stretches far beyond the issues specific to the individual pillars we have discussed. It is precisely because of this that it is such an intellectually stimulating subject and, indeed, why governments face such difficult challenges when trying to devise and implement effective social policy. Social policy matters because it has a real impact on real lives and tackles fundamental political questions about the nature of the good society. The different policy mechanisms that we have examined matter because they embody different goals and values, favour some groups over others, and influence the very nature of our societies. In other words, 'what' social policies look like matters. However, there also exists a very challenging academic question that goes beyond the 'What?' question of 'What do social policies do and look like?' that we have addressed here and, instead, asks the 'Why?' question: 'Why do different societies adopt different social policy solutions?' In drawing the book to a close, we want to briefly reflect on this 'Why?' question by highlighting some of the very significant political science work concerning the 'political economy of welfare' that has looked to address this question.

We have taken our lead in this book from Esping-Andersen (1990; see also Esping-Andersen, 1999) and we can do so here once again in tackling the 'Why?' question. His work was based on the theoretical proposition that the differences between welfare states – and the reason behind the three 'regimes' he identified – were the result of the balance of different political alliances that were made in each country based around the outcome of power struggles between social classes. This is why he called his 'three worlds' 'regimes', a term that has been widely and often wrongly used subsequently. His 'three worlds' are based not on empirical differences that he discovered in his data, but on his prior theory of class alliances.

Esping-Andersen argued that there are three basic types of welfare system: a liberal regime that offers minimal protection and little redistribution of income beyond providing a basic safety net, meaning that the levels of inequality generated by the market largely remain;

a social democratic regime that offers high levels of protection and redistributes income between social groups with the aim of creating a more equal society; and a conservative/corporatist regime that offers high levels of income protection, but only redistributes income between social classes on a modest scale.

More importantly for our purposes here, Esping-Andersen argued that each of these regimes was the outcome of specific historical and cultural conditions, with each nation leaning towards one regime or another on a more or less fixed basis. He showed, for example, that societies were more likely to develop a conservative welfare regime if Catholic political parties were comparably strong – that is, if they managed to gain a substantial number of parliamentary and cabinet seats on a regular basis – and if societies looked back at a comparably strong historical tradition of absolutism and authoritarianism. Meanwhile, he suggested that the relatively generous social security solutions in social democratic regime types were typically linked to working-class strength and, moreover, the ability of working-class groups to form lasting political coalitions with middle-class groups. For instance, Esping-Andersen suggested that it was the successful coalitions of Left and Agrarian parties in the Scandinavian countries that helped to broaden the support base – not least within the electorate – for the development of a comprehensive welfare state in those countries. Compared to the social democratic countries, working-class strength remained strictly limited in the liberal regime types. Consequently, the development of generous and universal social security solutions remained limited too. This, of course, is a rather crude summary of Esping-Andersen's thesis, but the key point for our purposes is to stress how important the *historical and cultural foundations* of a society are to the type of welfare system that develops. This argument is closely related to the discovery of the 'three worlds' by Esping-Andersen and more generally to the idea that there are *different solutions to welfare provision* in different nations.

Esping-Andersen's work is part of a more general theoretical stream emanating from political science that emphasises the *power resources* of opposing political groups as an explanation for the wide range of differing social policy frameworks found across nations. Power resource theories have long dominated the comparative and international analysis of social policies. Nevertheless, Esping-Andersen's findings – especially his classification of individual countries to one of the three welfare regime types – have not been uncontested. Esping-Andersen can be criticised for attaching too much importance in his theoretical position to class and class coalitions as a determining factor and also for his selective use of data – for example, he did not use housing in his analysis, perhaps because the housing data would not easily fit his threefold model. Not least, one has to keep in mind that his analysis only covers a relatively small number of high-income countries and was restricted to a single point in time.

We have to be careful not to impose his explanations on countries with completely different cultural, historical and economic traditions and on completely different times. We have seen the first attempts to develop alternative regime types for East Asian, Latin American and African countries around the world (see Gough and Wood, 2004; Walker and Wong, 2005) and to revisit the role of social policies for international social and economic development (Surender and Walker, 2013; Midgley, 2014). Many recent contributions on high-income democracies have questioned whether individual countries have shifted away from their historical policy settlements in response to the various longer-term policy challenges that governments have faced (Seeleib-Kaiser, 2008; Hacker and O'Leary, 2012; Kvist et al, 2012).

Power resource theories also play a major role in the so-called party difference hypotheses. Rather than concentrating on the strength of class coalitions, proponents of party difference explanations point to party-political dominance of the legislature and executive across countries (eg Castles, 1982; Huber and Stephens, 2001). So, for example, scholars would point to the fact that countries in which left-inclined social democratic parties were successful have had higher spending on welfare state services than those countries with longer-term right-wing or mixed party-political traditions. More refined versions of this very basic assumption have brought forward detailed theories about the very conditions necessary for such an influence to be discernible. The interdependence of left- and right-wing parties in their competition for electoral votes has been mentioned here. Equally, scholars have pointed to the important role that different political systems can play in shaping party influence (eg Immergut, 1992; Pierson, 1995). It is argued that it matters whether parties compete in a parliamentary or a presidential system, whether they compete in a federalist or a centralist system, and whether there are many or only a few parties – all these structural differences have an influence on the policy-making process, may favour certain interests over others and may therefore have an influence on the scope and functioning of the social pillars. These institutional approaches have gained much attention in contemporary debates about the reform of welfare states (Pierson, 2001) and have continued to do so after the recent global financial and economic crises (Farnsworth and Irving, 2011).

Closely related to institutional explanations of the development and change of the welfare pillars are explanations that emphasise policy inheritance or 'path dependency' (Hudson and Lowe, 2009; Pierson, 2004). For instance, as we have shown, the liberal, conservative and social democratic welfare regime types produce very dissimilar policy mechanisms; these dissimilarities are said to, in turn, produce repercussions for the policy-making process. So, for example, at the very start of the book, we began by describing the intense debate over healthcare reform in the US. Despite the fact that the healthcare system there is deemed inadequate by many – not least because it fails to provide coverage to millions of its citizens, including a large proportion of American children – the system has proved highly resistant to reform. In large part, this is because those who benefit most from the status quo – including the powerful private health insurance funds and private healthcare providers – are unlikely to endorse reforms that radically extend the role of the state and so threaten their role, their power and their profits. Yet, in many other countries, it is taken as a given that the state *should* be the main provider of healthcare, not least because the state has undertaken such a role for many decades. The broader theoretical argument here is that policy mechanisms can *shape* political interests, as well as reflecting them, and so early policy choices can be hard to change as a consequence. This is the main idea behind the notion that each nation's policies are often 'path-dependent': once they go down a particular direction of development, it can prove hard to reverse later.

Theoretical arguments of this sort are often omitted from introductory guides to social policy, but we introduce them here because we believe the 'Why?' questions matter as much as the 'What?' questions. Indeed, without a conceptual foundation, the mere comparison of data is not particularly meaningful – it is not possible to make true comparisons without some sort of theory. The emphasis in the previous chapters on the vast differences in the way in which the five pillars are organised and underpinned by different ideas of individuality, social solidarity and the role of the state across countries is very interesting in its own right. However, while we may be able to show how a number of countries differ in, say, their approach to child poverty or spending on health services, we are unable to say why they differ without some recourse to theory. While addressing the 'What?' questions – providing a guide map through the possibilities and limitations of social policy across the globe – is a sensible starting point for our tour of social policy, students interested in understanding the 'sense' behind the statistics and structural characteristics of comparative and international social policies have to take their short guide through social policy a stage further by considering the 'Why?' questions too.

Conclusion

All people across the world share more or less the same fundamental human needs; indeed, the belief that this is so underpins the Universal Declaration of Human Rights (United Nations General Assembly, 1948; see also www.un.org/en/documents/udhr/) that we have cited on various occasions throughout our discussion of the pillars of welfare. Modern social policies can play a hugely significant role in the delivery of human rights, but a key lesson highlighted in this book is that *how* this is achieved varies very considerably from country to country. Comparative welfare state research has shown that there are three or four basic models of provision but that each country has its own unique features. Moreover, we should not presume that social policies always meet essential human needs as fully as they might do or that the social rights of all people in a society are met equally: welfare states vary in their expansiveness and in the degree to which they aim to address social divisions and social inequalities.

In this book, we have emphasised the value of looking beyond a single country when thinking about social policy issues. The broader perspective that can be found by considering examples from different countries helps to sharpen our thinking about the nature of each pillar, the possibilities of social policy and the challenges that policy makers face. If you are German, American, Chinese or Brazilian – wherever you come from in fact – it can be natural to presume that the country you have experienced is the 'norm'. Looking at a range of different countries can usefully challenge presumptions about what is normal and what is possible. However, we have also emphasised here the importance of social theory in helping us to understand social policy. Facts and figures cannot tell us everything and an example taken out of context can be misleading too. We should not, therefore, be too simple-minded in our analysis of social policies. In particular, we should reflect on why nations differ and how far policy differences are a consequence of the long-run cultural, economic, political and institutional differences of nations. What this means in practice is that we should not presume that policies can easily be moved between nations: while, for instance, you might decide that Sweden, Denmark or Germany has a better social security policy framework than your own country, you should not necessarily conclude that your country should immediately adopt the approach found in one of those countries. Instead, you might want to first ask why the policy differences exist and to think about the broader factors that might lead your country to having what you regard as a less desirable policy framework.

Of course, in order to undertake such a reflection, you will most likely find it useful to extend your short tour of social policy into a much longer one. We should emphasise the point here once again that this short book is only a first step for readers new to this fascinating subject and we make no claim to have written a full, once-and-for-all account of social policy. At the start of the book, we said that our aim was to guide you through the main 'boulevards' of social policy and to point out the most famous 'tourist' sites. Just as any good guidebook ought to, we hope that our brief tour has whetted your appetite for a further trip to cover the other parts of the territory. The first time you visit a city, it is useful to know what the main buildings are called and where they are located, but much more can be gained on subsequent visits by scratching beneath this surface and learning more about the history of the buildings, the political debates that surrounded their construction or the social and environmental impacts of their construction. In exploring the five main pillars, we have given you a short overview of social policy. However, we concluded each chapter with an indication of some of the core readings that can take you further in your travels. We have now given you that first tour round the 'city' of social policy; we hope that we have inspired you to explore it further.

references

ABS (Australian Bureau of Statistics) (2013) *Life tables for Aboriginal and Torres Strait Islander Australians, 2010–2012*, Canberra: ABS, www.abs.gov.au/

Adams, R. (2002) *Social policy for social work*, Basingstoke: Palgrave.

Adams, R. (2010) *The short guide to social work*, Bristol: Policy Press.

Adema, W., Fron, P. and Ladaique, M. (2011) 'Is the European welfare state really more expensive? Indicators on social spending, 1980–2012; and a manual to the OECD Social Expenditure Database (SOCX)', OECD Social, Employment and Migration Working Papers No. 124.

Alcock, C., Daly, G. and Griggs, E. (2008) *Introducing social policy*, Abingdon: Routledge.

Alcock, P., M. May and S. Wright (eds) (2012) The student's companion to social policy, Oxford: Wiley-Blackwell.

Asthana, S. and Halliday, J. (2006) *What works in tackling health inequalities? Pathways, policies and practice through the lifecourse*, Bristol: Policy Press.

Bachelard, G. (1992) *The poetics of space*, Boston, MA: Beacon Press.

Baggott, R. (2007) *Understanding health policy*, Bristol: Policy Press.

Baggott, R. (2012) 'Health care', in P. Alcock, M. May and S. Wright (eds) *The student's companion to social policy*, Maldon, MA: Wiley-Blackwell, pp 331–7.

Baldock, J., L. Mitton, N. Manning and S. Vickerstaff (eds) (2012) *Social policy* (4th edn), Oxford: Oxford University Press.

Ball, S.J. (2013) *The education debate* (2nd edn), Bristol: Policy Press.

Bambra, C. (2005) 'Worlds of welfare and the health care discrepancy', *Social Policy & Society*, vol 4, no 1, pp 31–41.

Basit, T.N. and Tomlinson, S. (2014) *Social inclusion and higher education*, Bristol: Policy Press.

Béland, D. and Wadden, A. (2011) 'Social policy and the recent economic crisis in Canada and the United States', in K. Farnsworth and Z. Irving (eds) *Social Policy in challenging times. Economic crisis and welfare systems*, Bristol: Policy Press, pp 231–50.

Bettio, F. and Plantenga, J. (2004) 'Comparing care regimes in Europe', *Feminist Economics*, vol 10, pp 85–113.

Beveridge, W.H.B. (1942) *Social insurance and allied services*, Basingstoke: Macmillan.

Blakemore, K. and Warwick-Booth, L. (2013) *Social policy: an introduction*, Berkshire: Open University Press.

Blanden, J. and Macmillan, L. (2014) 'Education and intergenerational mobility: help or hindrance?', LSE Social Policy in a Cold Climate, Working Paper 8. http://sticerd.lse.ac.uk/dps/case/spcc/wp08.pdf

Blanden, J., Gregg, P. and Machin, S. (2005) *Intergenerational mobility in Europe and North America: a report supported by the Sutton Trust*, London: LSE Centre for Economic Performance.

Blank, R. and Burau, V. (2013) *Comparative health policy* (4th edn), Basingstoke: Palgrave Macmillan.

Bochel, H. and Daly, G. (2014) 'Education', in H. Bochel and G. Daly (eds) *Social policy*, Abingdon: Routledge, pp 249–66.

Bochel, H., Bochel, C., Page, R. and Sykes, R. (2009) *Social policy: themes, issues and debates*, Harlow: Pearson.

Bramley, G., Munro, M. and Pawson, H. (2004) *Key issues in housing: policies and markets in 21st-century Britain*, Basingstoke: Palgrave Macmillan.

Bureau of Justice Statistics (2011) 'Correctional populations in the United States, 2010', Bureau of Justice Statistics Bulletin, December, www.bjs.gov/content/pub/pdf/cpus10.pdf

Burnett, J. (1986) *A social history of housing, 1815–1985*, London: Routledge.

Callender, C. (2012) 'Lifelong learning and training', in P. Alcock, M. May and S. Wright (eds) *The student's companion to social policy*, Maldon, MA: Wiley-Blackwell, pp 345–51.

Castles, F.G. (1982) *The impact of parties: politics and policies in democratic capitalist states*, London: Sage.

Castles, F.G. (2007) *The disappearing state? Retrenchment realities in an age of globalization*, Cheltenham: Edward Elgar.

Colombo, F., Llena-Nozal, A., Mercier, J. and Tjadens, F. (2011) *Help wanted? Providing and paying for long-term care*, Paris: OECD.

Deacon, A. and Patrick, R. (2012) 'Employment', in P. Alcock, M. May and S. Wright (eds) *The student's companion to social policy*, Maldon, MA: Wiley-Blackwell, pp 324–30.

Donaldson, C. (2011) *Credit crunch health care. How economics can save our publicly-funded health services*, Bristol: Policy Press.

Dwyer, P. (2010) *Understanding social citizenship: themes and perspectives for policy and practice* (2nd edn), Bristol: Policy Press.

Eadie, T. and Morley, R. (2012) 'Crime, justice & punishment', in J. Baldock, L. Mitton, N. Manning and S. Vickerstaff (eds) *Social policy* (4th edn), Oxford: Oxford University Press, pp 369–94.

Edgar, B. (2009) *European review of statistics on homelessness*, Brussels: FEANTSA.

Edgar, B. and Meert, H. (2006) *Fifth review of statistics on homelessness*, Brussels: FEANTSA.

Esping-Andersen, G. (1990) *The three worlds of welfare capitalism*, Cambridge: Polity Press.

Esping-Andersen, G. (1999) *Social foundations of postindustrial economies*, Oxford: Oxford University Press.

European Commission (2003) 'Second Continuing Vocational Training Survey (detailed tables)', Luxembourg.

European Commission (2010) *Europe 2020: a strategy for smart, sustainable and inclusive growth*, Brussels: European Commission.

Eurostat (2014) 'Lifelong learning statistics'. http://ec.europa.eu/eurostat/statistics-explained/index.php/Lifelong_learning_statistics

Eurydice (2014) 'European encyclopedia of national education systems'. http://eacea.ec.europa.eu/education/eurydice/

Farnsworth, K. and Irving, Z. (2011) *Social policy in challenging times. Economic crisis and welfare systems*, Bristol: Policy Press.

Fitzpatrick, T. (2012) 'Cash transfers', in J. Baldock, L. Mitton, N. Manning and S. Vickerstaff (eds) *Social policy* (4th edn), Oxford: Oxford University Press, pp 217–38.

Förster, M. and d'Ercole, M. (2005) 'Income distribution and poverty in OECD countries in the second half of the 1990s', Social, Employment and Migration Working Papers, No. 22, OECD, Paris.

Giddens, A. (1991) *Modernity and self-identity: self and society in the late modern age*, Cambridge: Polity Press.

Glasby, J. (2012) 'Social care', in P. Alcock, M. May and S. Wright (eds) *The student's companion to social policy*, Maldon, MA: Wiley-Blackwell.

Glasby, J. and Daly, G. (2014) 'Adult health and social care', in H. Bochel and G. Daly (eds) *Social policy*, Abingdon, Routledge, pp 277–97.

Glennerster, H. (2003) *Understanding the finance of welfare: what reform costs and how to pay for it*, Bristol: Policy Press.

Gough, I. and Wood, G.D. (2004) *Insecurity and welfare regimes in Asia, Africa and Latin America: social policy in development contexts*, Cambridge: Cambridge University Press.

Greenberg, D. (2001) 'Novus Ordo Saeclorum? A commentary on Downes, and on Beckett and Western', *Punishment & Society*, vol 3, pp 81–93.

Griggs, E. (2014) 'Work and employment policy', in H. Bochel and G. Daly (eds) *Social policy*, Abingdon: Routledge, pp 225–43.

Grover, C. and Piggott, L. (2015) *Disabled people, work and welfare. Is employment really the answer?*, Bristol: Policy Press.

Hacker, J.S. and O'Leary, A. (2012) *Shared responsibility, shared risk: government, markets and social policy in the twenty-first century*, Oxford and New York, NY: Oxford University Press.

Ham, C. (2004) *Health policy in Britain: The politics and organisation of the National Health Service*, Basingstoke: Palgrave Macmillan.

Hazel, N. (2008) *Cross-national comparison of youth justice*, London: Youth Justice Board.

Hill, M. and Irving, Z. (2009) *Understanding social policy* (8th edn), Malden, MA: Wiley & Blackwell.

Holmans, A.E. (1987) *Housing policy in Britain: a history*, London: Croom Helm.

Holmans, A.E. (2000) 'British housing in the twentieth century: an end-of-century overview', in S. Wilcox (ed) *Housing finance review 1999–2000*, York: Joseph Rowntree Foundation, Chartered Institute of Housing and the Council of Mortgage Lenders.

Huber, E. and Stephens, J.D. (2001) *Development and crisis of the welfare state: parties and policies in global markets*, Chicago, IL: University of Chicago Press.

Huby, M. (1998) *Social policy and the environment*, Buckingham: Open University Press.

Hudson, J. and Lowe, S. (2009) *Understanding the policy process: analysing welfare policy and practice* (2nd edn), Bristol: Policy Press.

Hunter, D.J., Marks, L. and Smith, K. (2010) *The public health system in England*, Bristol: Policy Press.

IMF (International Monetary Fund) (2012) *Fiscal monitor: taking stock a progress report on fiscal adjustment*, Washington, DC: International Monetary Fund.

Immergut, E.M. (1992) *Health politics: interests and institutions in Western Europe*, Cambridge: Cambridge University Press.

Institute of Health Metrics and Evaluation (2014) 'Global Burden of Disease (GBD) data visualizations', www.healthdata.org/gbd/data-visualizations

ISSA (International Social Security Association) (2010) *Crisis country case study: United States*, ISSA Crisis Monitor Project, Geneva: International Social Security Association.

Jensen, C. (2008) 'Worlds of welfare services and transfers', *Journal of European Social Policy*, vol 8, no 2, pp 151–62.

Johnson, N. (1987) *The welfare state in transition: the theory and practice of welfare pluralism*, London: Harvester Wheatsheaf.

Kemeny, J. (1992) *Housing and social theory*, London: Routledge.

Kemeny, J. (2005) '"The really big trade-off" between home ownership and welfare: Castles' evaluation of the 1980 thesis, and a reformulation 25 years on', *Housing and Social Theory*, vol 22, no 2, pp 59–85.

Knepper, P. (2007) *Criminology and social policy*, London: Sage.

Kröger, T. and Yeandle, S. (2014) *Combining paid work and family care. Policies and experiences in international perspective*, Bristol: Policy Press.

Kvist, J., Fritzell, J., Hvinden, B. and Kangas, O. (2012) *Changing social equality. The Nordic welfare model in the 21st century*, Bristol: Policy Press.

Lewis, J. (2009) *Work–family balance, gender and policy*, Cheltenham: Edward Elgar.

Lowe, S. (2004) *Housing policy analysis: British housing in cultural and comparative context*, Basingstoke: Palgrave Macmillan.

Lowe, S. (2011) *The housing debate*, Bristol: Policy Press.

Lowe, S. and Tsenkova, S. (2003) *Housing change in East and Central Europe: integration or fragmentation*, Aldershot: Ashgate.

Marshall, T.H. (1950) *Citizenship and social class: and other essays*, Cambridge: Cambridge University Press.

Mayosi, B.M. and Benatar, S.R. (2014) 'Health and health care in South Africa – 20 years after Mandela', *The New England Journal of Medicine*, vol 371, no 14, pp 1344–53.

McKay, S. and Rowlingson, K. (2012) 'Income maintenance and social security', in P.Alcock, M. May and S.Wright (eds) *The student's companion to social policy*, Maldon, MA: Wiley-Blackwell.

McKeown, T. (1979) *The role of medicine: dream, mirage or nemesis?*, Oxford: Blackwell.

Midgley, J. (2014) *Social development: theory and practice*, London: Sage.

Millar, J. (ed) (2009) *Understanding social security*, Bristol: Policy Press.

Millar, J. and Haux, T. (2012) 'Family policy', in P. Alcock, M. May and S. Wright (eds) *The student's companion to social policy*, Maldon, MA: Wiley-Blackwell.

Mortimore, P. (2014) *Education under siege. Why there is a better alternative*, Bristol: Policy Press.

Muncie, J. and Goldson, B. (2006) 'States of transition', in J. Muncie and B. Goldson (eds) *Comparative youth justice*, London: Sage.

Munro, E. and Manful, E. (2010) *Safeguarding children: a comparison of England's data with that of Australia, Norway and the United States*, Department for Education Research Report DFE-RR198, London: Department for Education.

Nettleton, S. (2006) *The sociology of health and illness*, Cambridge: Polity Press.

Newburn, T. (2012a) 'Criminal justice', in P.Alcock, M. May and S.Wright (eds) *The student's companion to social policy*, Maldon, MA: Wiley-Blackwell, pp 366–74.

Newburn, T. (2012b) *Criminology* (2nd edn), London: Routledge.

OECD (Organisation for Economic Co-operation and Development) (2013) *Pensions at a glance 2013*, Paris: OECD.

OECD (2014a) *Benefits and wages: statistics*, Paris: OECD, www.oecd.org/els/benefits-and-wages-statistics.htm

OECD (2014b) *Benefits and wages: country specific information*, Paris: OECD, www.oecd.org/social/soc/benefits-and-wages-country-specific-information.htm

OECD (2014c) *OECD family database*, Paris: OECD, www.oecd.org/social/family/database.htm

OECD (2014d) *Society at a glance 2014*, Paris: OECD.

OECD (2014e) *Economic outlook*, Paris: OECD.

OECD (2014f) *Programme for International Student Assessment 2014*, Paris: OECD Publishing.

OECD (2014g) *Education at a glance: OECD indicators*, Paris: OECD Publishing.

OECD (2014h) *Health at a glance*, Paris: OECD Publishing.

ONS (2014) 'Life expectancies (detailed tables)'. http://ons.gov.uk/ons/taxonomy/index.html?nscl=Life+Expectancies

Pahl, J. (2012) 'The family and welfare', in J. Baldock, L. Mitton, N. Manning and S. Vickerstaff (eds) *Social policy* (4th edn), Oxford: Oxford University Press, pp 125–50.

Pascall, G. (2012) 'Health and health policy', in J. Baldock, L. Mitton, N. Manning and S. Vickerstaff (eds) *Social policy* (4th edn), Oxford: Oxford University Press, pp 260–284.

Payne, C.S. (2013) 'Expenditure on healthcare in the UK: 2011', ONS.

Pfaller, A., Gough, I. and Therborn, G. (1991) *Can the welfare state compete? A comparative study of five advanced capitalist countries*, Basingstoke: Macmillan.

Pierson, P. (1995) 'Fragmented welfare states: federalism and the development of social policy', *Governance*, vol 8, pp 449–78.

Pierson, P. (2001) *The new politics of the welfare state*, Oxford: Oxford University Press.

Pierson, P. (2004) *Politics in time: history, institutions, and social analysis*, Princeton, NJ: Princeton University Press.

Powell, M. (2007) *Understanding the mixed economy of welfare*, Bristol: Policy Press.

Powell, M. (2014) 'Health policy', in H. Bochel and G. Daly (eds) *Social policy*, Abingdon: Routledge, pp 349–70.

Priestley, M. (2012) 'Disability', in P. Alcock, M. May and S. Wright (eds) *The student's companion to social policy*, Maldon, MA: Wiley-Blackwell, pp 405–11.

Prison Reform Trust (2013) 'Prison: the facts', Bromley Briefings, Summer, www.prisonreformtrust.org.uk/Portals/0/Documents/Prisonthefacts.pdf

Rose, R. (2005) *Learning from comparative public policy: a practical guide*, London: Routledge.

Roulstone, A. and Prideaux, S. (2012) *Understanding disability policy*, Bristol: Policy Press.

Seeleib-Kaiser, M. (2008) *Welfare state transformations. Comparative perspectives*, Basingstoke: Palgrave Macmillan.

Shildrick, T., MacDonald, R., Webster, C. and Garthwaite, K. (2012) *Poverty and insecurity. Life in low-pay, no-pay Britain*, Bristol: Policy Press.

Smith, G.D. (2003) *Health inequalities: lifecourse approaches*, Bristol: Policy Press.

Smith, J.C. and Medalia, C. (2014) 'Health insurance coverage in the United States: 2013', Current Population Reports, US Census Bureau.

Smith S.J. and Searle B.A. (eds) (2010) *A Blackwell companion to the economics of housing; the housing wealth of nations*, Oxford and Malden, MA: Wiley-Blackwell.

Snell, C. and Haq, G. (2014) *The short guide to environmental policy*, Bristol: Policy Press.

Spicker, P. (2011) *How social security works*, Bristol: Policy Press.

Surender, R. and Walker, R. (2013) *Social policy in a developing world*, Cheltenham: Edward Elgar.

Sutherland, R. (2013) *Education and social justice in a digital age*, Bristol: Policy Press.

Sykes, R. (2012) 'Economic policy and social policy', in P. Alcock, M. May and S. Wright (eds) *The student's companion to social policy*, Maldon, MA: Wiley-Blackwell, pp 153–9.

Tawney, R.H. (1931) *Equality*, London: Allen & Unwin.

Titmuss, R.M. (1956) *The social division of welfare*, Liverpool: Liverpool University Press.

UNDP (United Nations Development Programme) (2014) *Human Development Report 2014. Sustaining human progress: reducing vulnerabilities and building resilience*, New York, NY: UNDP, www.undp.org/

Unesco (United Nations Educational, Scientific, and Cultural Organization) and Unicef (United Nations Children's Fund) (2013) *Envisioning education in the post-2015 development agenda*, New York, NY: Unicef.

UNICEF (United Nations Children's Fund) (2007) *Child poverty in perspective: an overview of child well-being in rich countries*, Innocenti Report Card 7, Florence: UNICEF Innocenti Research Centre.

UNICEF (2013) *Child well-being in rich countries: a comparative overview*, UNICEF Innocenti Report Card 11, Florence: UNICEF Office of Research.

UNICRI (United Nations Interregional Crime and Justice Research Institute) (2000) 'International crime victims survey: key findings', www.unicri.it/services/library_documentation/publications/icvs/statistics/

United Nations General Assembly (1948) *Universal Declaration of Human Rights*, Lake Success, NY: United Nations Department of Public Information.

UNODC (United Nations Office on Drugs and Crime) (2011) *Cannabis: a short review*, New York, NY: UNODC.

UNDP (United Nations Development Programme) (2014) Human development report 2014. *Sustaining human progress: Reducing vulnerabilities and building resilience*, New York: UNDP. www.undp.org

Valentine, G. (2001) *Social geographies: Society and space*, Harlow: Longman.

Vickerstaff, S. (2012a) 'Education, schools and training', in J. Baldock, L. Mitton, N. Manning and S. Vickerstaff (eds) *Social policy* (4th edn), Oxford: Oxford University Press, pp 239–59.

Vickerstaff, S. (2012b) 'Work and welfare', in J. Baldock, L. Mitton, N. Manning and S. Vickerstaff (eds) *Social policy* (4th edn), Oxford: Oxford University Press, pp 100–24.

Vickerstaff, S., Phillipson, C. and Wilkie, R. (2012) *Work, health and wellbeing: the challenges of managing health at work*, Bristol: Policy Press.

Wacquant, L. (2009) *Punishing the poor: the neoliberal government of social insecurity*, London: Duke University Press.

Walker, A. and Wong, C.-k. (2005) *East Asian welfare regimes in transition: from Confucianism to globalisation*, Bristol: Policy Press.

Weishaupt, T. (2014) 'Central steering and local autonomy in public employment services', PES to PES Dialogue, The European Commission Mutual Learning Programme for Public Employment Services.

West, A. (2012) 'Education and schools', in P. Alcock, M. May and S. Wright (eds) *The student's companion to social policy*, Maldon, MA: Wiley-Blackwell, pp 338–44.

WHO (World Health Organisation) (2014) 'World Health Organisation statistical information system', www.who.int/whosis/en/index.html

Wincup, E. (2013) *Understanding crime and social policy*, Bristol: Policy Press.

World Bank (2014) 'World development indicators'. http://data.worldbank.org/data-catalog/world-development-indicators

Index